LIFE SUCKS

A Bloodsucker's Blog

ELLA STONE

Also by Ella Stone

Dark Creatures Prequel Novellas

Mother of Wolves

Son of a Vampire

Man and Wolf

Call of the Grimoire

The Dark Creatures Saga

Dark Creatures

Dark Destiny

Dark Deception

Dark Redemption

Dark Reckoning

The Bloodsuckers Blog Series

Life Sucks

Love Bites

Lost Souls

First published 2022

Darkerside Publications

ISBN: 978-1-915346-08-7

Edited by Carol Worwood

Cover by Orina Kafe Digital Art & Cover Design

Chapter 1

Date: March 2nd
Followers: 0
Time: 8:00 p.m.

FUCK. Seriously. Fuck. This is not what I agreed to. Not even close.

Shit.

I need to breathe. I need to breathe and keep talking. Or tranquillise myself. I could do that. I could shoot myself in the side with one of the sedatives I've got in my bag. But then what? I just lie here unconscious until it wears off and hope that no one comes in?

SHIT!!!!

Breathe Merrewyn. Deep breath in. Deep breath out.

Deep breath in. Deep breath out. Screw that. I'm just going to keep typing.

In case you're asking yourself why I'm having a full-on breakdown, hiding in my best friend's spare bedroom with the lights off, it's because I'm at her FUCKING ENGAGEMENT PARTY! Yes, a party. Not some quiet little get-together where I can slowly reintroduce myself to polite society. Not some intimate gathering where I get to take my time and casually mention that I need her to hook me up with a bag of blood each month so that I don't become a raging murder machine.

I should have run away. I should have got right back in the lift and out to the car the moment I saw what I was walking into. Seriously, I can't believe it. This is a disaster waiting to happen.

Oh, I'm Merrewyn by the way, but you can call me Ryn. And I guess this is now my blog.

Chapter 2

Date: March 2nd
Followers: 0
Time: 8:40 p.m.

YOU'RE PROBABLY WONDERING how I ended up here, starting a blog in the spare room of my best friend's apartment well, actually, my only friend, who I haven't seen in five years. And maybe you're now wondering why it's been so long. In case that wasn't obvious from my last post, I'm a vampire. You know. Immortal. Ageless. Sharp pointy teeth. Definite aversion to the sun. Drink human blood to sustain my existence. All of that. However, I'm currently facing the prospect of a severe shortage of that particular refreshment.

I've been a vampire since I was seventeen (which was seven years ago), and until recently getting blood had not been an issue, as my mum had a steady job as a doctor at a small surgery and ran monthly blood-donation sessions to ensure our fridge stayed well stocked. (Just to make it clear, most of the donations went to the hospital, she just pilfered a couple of bags each time to keep me going.) Last week though, all that changed.

Attendance at family dinners is non-negotiable in our house, despite the fact that I don't eat. But it keeps my parents happy. So, every night, we gather around the kitchen table together. (Sometimes I discretely drink half pint of blood from a metal bottle, but I don't need to feed every day, so most of the time I'm just there to watch them eat. Great, right?)

So, we were in our kitchen which is massive, draughty and utterly outdated. Think eighties. Beige and brown lino flooring, wooden cabinets and foul yellow tiles. For the last couple of years, Mum has been desperate to get the decorators in but thought better of it, just in case they weren't the only ones to get peckish while they were working here.

The house overlooks farm and woodland at the front, with more farmland and a couple of crumbling old barns at the back and then more woods beyond them. Honestly, this is the type of place that horror-film directors would wet themselves over. And Instagrammers too, what with all the open fields and stuff. We don't get to appreciate the view, however, as the curtains are usually closed. You know, with me being a vampire and everything.

Anyway, back to the story. Normally, dinner is a fairly casual affair. We talk over one another. I mope about how much I miss being human, while simultaneously refusing any suggestion that I leave the house, and Glen talks about being captain of the school rugby team or all the various awards he's won and how he got top marks in his assessments and every university wants to offer him a place. Mum often tries to persuade me to go late-night shopping with her or take a trip to the cinema. And Dad, well he normally has his head buried in a massive book.

This particular day last week, there was none of that. Glen was scrolling on his phone, studying for a test, and Dad was practically asleep in his chair despite it only being seven o'clock. But it was Mum's behaviour that caught my attention. The way her heart was hammering. (Yes, I could hear it.) And the way her hands were fidgeting. The smell of adrenaline that was coming from her was strong enough to give me a head rush. Despite his lack of heightened senses, Glen also finally picked up on the vibe and asked her if something was wrong.

"It's the Council," she said. "They're closing the surgery."

At this point, Dad was wide awake again, and all eyes were on her.

"They'll relocate me," she said, her voice almost

breaking. "Somewhere not too far, probably, but I won't be in charge of blood donations anymore. It may take me months to be in a position to you know …"

"Steal the literal lifeblood of good Samaritans?" I offered.

"Yes, although I'm not sure I'd phrase it quite like that."

An eerie silence descended on us. My family is never silent.

"Well, it's not exactly the end of the world, is it?" I said, trying to lift the mood with the perkiest voice I could manage. (I am not a perky person. Just putting that out there right now.) "I can manage on two pints a month. There must be half-a-dozen bags in the freezer, right? And a couple in the fridge, too. I'll just cut down and put you guys on rotation."

This felt like a logical solution to me, but Mum, Glen and Dad exchanged looks, making me realise I was missing something.

"Do you read all the information I research for you?" Mum asked, her eyes one hundred percent focused back on me.

"Yes. Of course."

I'm a useless liar and some things don't change just because you're dead. Their eyes were all still locked on me, so I tried again, adding a half-shrug.

"I've read most of them. Well, some of them. Like, I skim read them."

As their gazes bored into me with a new level of intensity, I let out a heavy sigh. Most of what I'm supposed to look at is in a massive pile on my bedroom floor, unread and gathering dust. What can I say, they're just not as appealing as SJ Maas.

"Fine, I find them really dull. They're about rats and blood counts and I really don't care that much. I am what I am. What difference is me reading a two-thousand-word article on the behaviour of rats after ingesting my venom going to make?"

I'm not sure what kind of answer I expected, but I didn't get any. Instead, Mum and Glen pressed their lips together in tight lines, while my dad stared at the remaining food on his plate.

"You really should read them," Glen eventually said.

"If you don't get enough blood, your body will start to shut down, and eventually you could even start to desiccate," my mum explained.

"Basically, you need at least four pints a month if you are going to remain a functioning being," Glen added. "I'm going to uni in September and if Mum doesn't find another source, then you'll be down to two donors. You can't survive on that. This is bad news, Ryn. Really bad news."

Just so you are aware, the average person can only safely lose a pint of blood once every three months or so. It doesn't take a maths genius to work out that the numbers didn't stack up. *Really bad news* might be putting it mildly.

I turned to Dad, hoping he'd have something insightful or positive to say. He's a mythologist, meaning he knows more about legendary creatures than pretty much anyone else, except my mother and other vampires. After all the experiments she has done on me over the years, she's definitely the expert on my kind. Dad opened his mouth to speak, but no words came out.

"Okay, it will be tough, but I'll manage?" I said. "I'm a vampire. I can survive anything. I'll stay alive until we find a solution."

"But we probably won't," my father said, quietly.

My head snapped in his direction, but he was still staring down at his plate as if it would take a superhuman effort to even lift his head up. So instead, I looked to Mum.

"What does he mean?" I said.

The silence stretched out between us although to give Glen his due, he managed to steady his pulse by a fraction.

"You'll likely be overwhelmed by blood lust and murder us all," my mother said matter-of-factly.

"Unless they chain you up," Glen added. "And even then you could break free."

"No!"

I could feel myself shaking. The air (that I technically

don't need) was getting thin around me, and quicker than anyone could blink, I was on my feet, hands on the table, fangs out.

"Why did no one tell me? Why did no one tell me this?"

"I gave you the information to read, darling," my mother said, as if this was a defence.

"This is something you *tell* someone!" I screamed, loud enough to shake the cutlery on the table. "You don't give them a massive stack of paper without, you know, a quick side note. *Darling, check appendix six. That tells you when you're most likely to kill us.*"

"You are a vampire, pumpkin," Dad said, not the slightest bit diplomatically. "There's always been a risk of you attacking us."

"Great. This is fucking great."

Normally, I get yelled at for swearing, despite the fact that I'm technically twenty-four, but even Mum stayed silent this time. My head was spinning. No one was eating. My cup of blood was starting to clot, and their pasta was congealing to the same consistency.

"We need to find more donors," Glen said, quietly. "I bet Lovisa would be one. What do you say? We could take a road trip."

Road trip. To most people, those words would probably conjure up visions of happy camping holidays and scenic tours around the countryside. I can only think of the one time I left the house since I was turned, when I lost control and ended up attacking a stranger. And trust me, that's not something I'm in a hurry to repeat.

Chapter 3

Date: March 2nd
Followers: 2
Time: 9:10 p.m.
Hours stuck in this room: 2.5

THIS IS TURNING out to be strangely cathartic. And I can't believe I've already got two followers. It's crazy. I only posted the last blog ten minutes ago. I guess I might as well carry on. I've got nothing else to do. I can hear the laughter and music coming from downstairs, and there's no way I'm facing that. Drinking the blood of the other guests at Lovisa's engagement party would be a sure way to get my wedding invite revoked, so I'm staying put. I tried pacing the room for a minute, to see if

I could calm my nerves that way, but I felt like a freaking caged animal. So I'm back writing another one of these posts. And for as long as my phone has battery life, I can tell you a bit more about what's going on with me. I guess there's quite a lot to fill you in on, after all.

Seven years ago, I was an average girl, living an average life.

Actually, no. Scrap that. That's not technically true. I was far from average. As a young kid, I suffered from leukaemia, and trust me, if you know anyone who's gone through that, it's safe to say that they are not average. They are fucking hardcore. They're superheroes. They're warriors. Seriously. They're called survivors for a reason. And I was one of those. I was a freaking survivor.

But by the time I was seventeen, those days were behind me. I was normal again and that was exactly how I wanted it. I went to school, had a cat, Loki (who we still have, actually), and a freaking perfect boyfriend named Fin. And that's how I thought life would go on, forever. But that all changed when we went on an outing.

Most families get theme parks and zoos and fun places like that on their days out together. We got random caves and megalithic monuments, thanks to Dad. Visiting ancient Neolithic ruins was the type of exciting trip we went on, and the place that he took us to that day was no different. Apparently, the ruins that we were traipsing over were the remains of one of the first churches ever built in the UK and he wanted to see if there was any mythological stuff going on there. (I've already told you that's his thing, right? Myths and stuff. If I keep doing this blog, I'll maybe do a post about it later. Though, trust me, it won't be half as much fun as you might imagine.)

Obviously, I had no interest in yet another derelict building and was ambling apathetically around, texting Lovisa and Fin. Maybe if I had been paying attention I would have noticed that the part of the ruins I was walking on was even more dilapidated and treacherous than the rest of the site. Maybe I would have watched where I was going a little more carefully. Maybe I would know exactly what occurred.

Neither of my parents were close when the accident happened. Dad was off reading some inscriptions, trying to decide if there were any hidden messages in them. Mum was taking photos of the landscape, and Glen was doing whatever twelve-year-old boys do.

According to Mum, there was a massive crash. She turned around, and I was on the ground. Dropping her camera, she ran over the ruins, screaming my name, and then Dad and Glen started doing the same. But given that they were all spread out on the other side of the site, it took them a few moments to get over to where I was.

When they reached me, I was unconscious. Pinned to my chest was a bag of blood and a note, which read:

Feed her this. You know what she is now.

Freaky or what?

But the freaky doesn't end there. The whole time we had been at the site we hadn't seen another person, not one. Which isn't really surprising given the number of infinitely better things people could have been doing with a sunny Saturday afternoon. But Glen swore than when he was running towards me, he saw a woman. Mum and Dad are certain they didn't. For years they tried to convince him that he must have imagined her, but I don't think he did. After all, someone turned me. Someone made me what I am.

By the time I came around, Mum had concealed the note and blood in her bag. It wasn't until later that they explained what had happened. At the time, all I cared about was that my phone had been smashed. That was a big deal. Fin had planned our first ever weekend away for my eighteenth birthday the following month, and Lovisa and I had been busy discussing all the details. (I'll let you imagine those texts, but I will say they involved me and him and some seriously gorgeous underwear that I didn't plan on wearing all night.) But now I couldn't even message them. Anyway, that was my main concern.

"Where's my phone?" were the first words out of my mouth, followed by, "What the … I'll have to get it fixed."

"We should get home straight away," Mum said, helping me to my feet.

"Shouldn't we take her to the hospital?" Glen asked.

Given that Mum is a doctor, she was obviously the

one who knew best. Dad and Glen looked at her, waiting for her answer.

"Merrewyn, keep your head still and follow my finger," she said, holding one out and moving it from side to side. "Okay, now look into the light."

She did a few more random checks, but there was no sign of any damage at all—literally no sign. Not even a scratch anywhere.

"We'll head home, but I'll keep an eye on you. If you feel funny at all, you need to tell me."

Funny. Yeah, that's putting it mildly.

"What about my phone? I was texting Lovisa?" I said, feeling absolutely fine and still not concerned with anything else.

"I'm sure we'll be able to fix it," Mum said, ushering me forwards towards my dad.

The blood craving (obviously I didn't know that's what it was then), didn't set in for a couple of hours, there was just this intense grogginess. When we got in, Mum suggested I head up to my room and put a film on, and I remember walking upstairs feeling like my feet weren't part of my body. And the sounds. Everything was so damn loud. Every time someone shouted on the television it was like a bullet though my skull. Glen tapping away on his computer in the next room felt like he was hammering nails into my temples. Eventually I gave up and went downstairs, thinking I should perhaps tell Mum that something wasn't quite right.

In the kitchen, I poured myself a glass of water from the tap and the rushing sound made my eardrums shake. But that was nothing compared to how it tasted. Putrid is probably the best word to describe it. Utterly putrid.

"What are you doing?" Glen asked, coming into the room "You're making a weird noise."

"No I'm not," I replied, but my voice came out hoarse, more like a snarl. But that was only half of it. The second I opened my mouth, fangs appeared! I swear I will never forget the pain of them piercing my gums.

"Glen, upstairs!" Mum yelled, pushing him away from me.

"But!"

"Now!" Her eyes were locked on my mouth. "Steven, where's that bag? Get the blood!"

My father hesitated. For all his knowledge of the mythological, he was stunned by the sight of a real vampire in his kitchen.

"Are you sure about this, Angela. It's just … unbelievable," he muttered, taking a step towards me, but Mum pushed him aside and grabbed the bag from the fridge herself and shoved it into my hands. I drank down every drop without even pausing for breath, and when I was done, Mum shot me with a tranquilliser from her doc's bag. Yup, you read that right. A needle straight to the neck. The first of many as it happened. And that's it. My life has never been the same since.

Now for the real kicker. You read earlier that I'd been

sick as a kid, right? Well, eight days before I was turned, I'd had a hospital appointment to check that it hadn't come back. And what do you know? I was completely clear. Fully healthy without of trace of cancer. And yet I died anyway. Thanks life. You really threw a curve ball there.

So that almost brings us to why I'm here, hiding in Lovisa's spare bedroom.

I need more blood. I can't survive on just my parents and occasionally Glen's, and Lovisa is the only other person who knows what I am. She's also seen exactly what I'm capable of.

Chapter 4

Date: March 2nd
Followers: 4
Time: 9:30 p.m.
Hours stuck in this room: 3-ish

SORRY ABOUT THAT. I heard people coming upstairs. (Yes, this London penthouse is so posh it has two levels. Not to mention massive floor-to-ceiling windows that have inbuilt electric blinds which, along with the lights, are voice activated.) Anyway, I heard footsteps and I freaked out that they were about to come in here. I held onto the door handle, and they fortunately assumed the room was locked. One good thing about being a vampire is super strength; no one's getting past me if I don't want them to.

You might also have noticed I've added a time thingy to the top of the page. Given that I'm going to be trapped here a while—I can't go anywhere as there are so many people blocking my route out—it felt like something else to do.

I still need to talk to Lovisa about why I'm really here.

Unexpectedly, I now have four followers. How cool is that? And you four must have a lot of questions, too. So, seeing as I am practically a penthouse prisoner, I might as well answer them.

ARE YOU SUPER STRONG?

Easy one to start with. Yes, actually, I really am and not just the holding-a-door-shut-so-no-one-can-get-in type strong. I've lost count of the number I've pulled off their hinges. My drum kit is custom made with reinforced steel and I once gave Glen a compound fracture during a game of Monopoly. (Family board games are banned now.) I can bench press over 500kg and can even lift a tractor. (That's a test I did with Glen, not Mum, btw.) And I can unscrew any jar lid, although that often ends up with the jar broken, too.

It seems that the more blood I consume the more my vampire powers increase. Also, we found out from testing rats that the strength I get from drinking out of blood bags is nothing compared to what it would be if I drank Direct Blood (DB), by which I mean straight from the vein. I'm pretty sure one of you is going to ask why I don't do that, but honestly, it's not like I need that much strength to operate the TV remote. Besides, my fangs have venom in them, and so far we're not too sure what the long-term effects of repeated exposure to the venom would be on my donors. (We discovered what the short-term ones are when Glen convinced me to let him touch my fangs, but that's another story.) So, right now, we drain my venom each morning, and Mum puts it in with the medical waste at work.

Anyway, back to your other questions.

DOES YOUR MUM HAVE VAMPIRE RATS AND CAN THEY MAKE VAMPIRE HUMANS TOO?

I like the fact we've got a scientific question about Mum's studies, unless you're planning on unleashing a hoard of vampire rats in the hope that they'll turn everyone on the planet into blood-sucking, light-afflicted half beings. In which case, I'm a little concerned. Still, I should answer the question. Yes and No. In that order. There are a few differences with the rats. Unlike me, their hearts still beat but only at a rate of about 4 times per minute. As opposed to my zero count. This might be why they continue to age with a near normal lifespan and also maintain a core temperature, which I don't, although it's substantially lower than their living counterparts. They do have increased abilities and only ingest blood, but we keep the amount low so they don't get too strong. It took Mum several years of generational breeding to get to this stage, and they are now sufficiently similar to me for her to run tests on. And secondly, no. They can't transfer their vampirism to humans, only to each other. Just like I can't transfer mine to them by biting them. (Please don't ask me how I know that. Work it out for yourselves.)

IS YOUR MUM LICENSED TO TEST ON RATS?

So, sticking with the rats then. Let's not worry about the vampire girl suffering from agoraphobia but the legalities of my mother and her animal testing. The truth is, I have no idea. Do you need a licence for testing on rats? Probably.

The thing is, thanks to her experiments, we've found out way more about me than would otherwise have been possible. For example, we know that a bite isn't enough to turn someone into a vampire. The venom in my teeth is only a catalyst. The person would need to have vampire blood in their system when their heart is still pumping. And, as we have already discussed, if I don't get Lovisa on side with blood donations, I'm likely to go fully psycho vamp. So, whether Mum does or doesn't have a licence for the rat testing, I'm going to have to say I'm not that concerned. Selfish? Perhaps a little. But if what she learns stops me attacking innocent people, we should all take that as a win. Now, moving on.

CAN I GO OUT IN SUNLIGHT?

This does not have a black-and-white answer. Can I? Yes. Should I? Possibly not. Sunlight doesn't cause me to burst into flames or turn into a block of stone. Well, not straight away. First comes the headache. Sounds lame, but it's not. It attacks my temples and behind my eye sockets. It feels like my whole head is going to explode, and it comes on fast. Just a few seconds in midday sun, and I can't even see. I can't swallow. I can't think. That might not sound like much, but it's crap, believe me. And then there's the skin issue, of course. Yeah, that one's a biggie.

The best way to describe it, as Mum has told me this repeatedly, is photosensitivity. It's also what she's told every person we ever knew when giving a reason for us moving to the back of beyond. Including love-of-my-life-now-gone-forever-ex-boyfriend, Fin (although this is not the time to get into that). Whatever you call the condition, it's not pleasant. Basically, the energy in the UV rays that come from the sun (photons if you want the technical name), is too intense for my skin to deal with, so it starts burning up and fast. Imagine fat in a frying pan. That's pretty much what happens. Yes, I heal quicker than the average person—an answer to another of your questions—but that doesn't change the fact that having every inch of your skin breaking out in huge blistering boils is more than a tad uncomfy. Sure, I can put sunscreen on, factor 100, and that helps, but to be honest, it's not like I ever go out. And I'm fine with that.

DO I KNOW ANY OTHER VAMPIRES?

This one sucks to answer. I do not. Not one. Nada. And I hate it. The rational part of me understands that anonymity is key when it comes to being a vampire, so they don't exactly publicise their existence. And trust me, I've looked. I spent a large chunk of my fourth year searching for them. In fact, I became obsessed with trying to find other vamps.

It coincided with the height of Glen's computer-nerd stage. Under my supervision, he would hack into various police databases to try and find leads to follow. Our main search criteria concerned finding animal attacks that had left victims disorientated or with memory loss (one of the side effects of the venom), or worse still, bodies found with unknown toxins in their system (i.e. vampire venom). We found a couple of cases that fitted, and Mum even went to track them down, but all were dead ends. So no, I don't know any other vampires, but they must be out there, because it was one who turned me.

HAVE YOU EVER KILLED ANYONE?

Wow. Not pulling your punches are you? The answer is no … but I have got damn close, and trust me, it was seriously scary. It's not something I like to think about, but as I'm in self-imposed quarantine right now, and it sounds like they just got the karaoke machine out downstairs, I might as well confess. I'm telling you everything else, after all. All four of you. So here it is. My first ever recounting of the time I nearly murdered someone.

My first years of being a vampire were seriously shitty and not just because of the whole craving-human-blood issue. My parents packed us up and moved us to the massive, creepy farmhouse we now live in. It's surrounded by acres and acres of fields so that no one is going to accidentally turn up at our door and provide me with a fresh home-delivery service. I had to leave my friends, my old life. I had to leave Fin.

By the time I become a vampire, Fin and I had been together for two years. We met through his younger brother, Noah, who was the guitarist in the band I used to play with. (Yup, I was a cool human, even if I'm a mundane vampire.) Fin was a year older than me and two years older than Noah. He was the quiet, brooding type and used to sit and read while he waited for Noah to finish practising. Little by little, we got talking, and after a couple of months, I asked him out. The rest, as they say, is history. We were inseparable. I mean that. If we went a single weekend without seeing each other you could bet we sent at least a hundred-and-fifty text messages between us. He knew everything about me, as I did about him. He wasn't my first kiss, but he was the first guy I did anything more than kiss with. Honestly, I truly believed he was my soul mate. Which was why I thought he would come looking for me after my parents drugged me up to the eyeballs, packed up our things and moved us to our new place. Well, I couldn't have been more wrong.

For reasons they thought best, they banned me from any sort of social media or contact with the outside world during the first couple of years, and it made my loneliness all the more unbearable. As such, I slipped into a seriously dark place.

About a year PD (post death), I was not doing well. I

had gone nearly two months without drinking a thing. I refused point blank. I just wanted to be with Fin. My mother was sedating me nearly every day, before I could get violent and attack her, and my skin took on this really eerie translucency while my fangs were permanently on display. I didn't even care if I dried up and died for a second time. I honestly felt like I had nothing left to live for. But the thing is, in times like that, just the tiniest spark of light can illuminate the positive. And Glen, well, he provided that spark.

Given my enhanced hearing, I knew he was approaching my door before he even knocked.

"Go away," I yelled, groggy from the sedatives, not that my responses back then were much more creative no matter how awake I was.

"Okay," he said, but opened the door a crack and threw something in before closing it quickly and returning to his room. Given his age and somewhat disturbing sense of humour, I imagined it was going to be anything from a frog, or a rat from Mum's lab, to a stink bomb, but it only took me a second to see that the item that had landed on my bed was a phone.

Like I said, Mum and Dad had been crazily strict about me having no communication with anyone up to this point. No internet access. Not even for Netflix. Seriously, I had to watch DVDs or, worse still, regular TV. I had no idea what was going on and I just stared at it for a moment. Then there came a familiar voice.

"Hello? Hello? Is someone there? Who is this?"

"Lovisa?"

I grabbed the phone and pressed it to my ear.

"Is that you? Is that really you?"

The sound of her voice made me feel like I was taking the first breath since the moment I had changed. Every fibre of my body felt alive.

"Ryn? Oh my God, Ryn! I've missed you so much. Where are you? Are you okay? What happened to you? Please, tell me everything."

And then, rather than leading with the lie about developing photosensitivity and being sick, I told her the truth. All of it. I told her what I had become. It was amazing. I felt free and unburdened. From then on we spoke all the time. I couldn't be with her physically, but I was able to talk honestly with someone outside my family at last, and also I'll admit, it was good to be able to live vicariously through her to some degree. For the first time in a long while, I was happy. But then I did something stupid. Seriously stupid. Which is how—

Chapter 5

Date: March 2nd
Followers: 6
Time: 10 p.m.
Hours stuck in this room: 3.5

SORRY, my phone just ran out of battery. I just had time to hit post. I should have realised it was getting low. Thankfully, Lovisa popped in only a couple of minutes later to check on me.

"I am so, so sorry," she said pulling me in for a hug.

It was strange having such close contact with someone other than family. I could hear her heart beating and smell the blood pumping in her veins. It was more enticing than fresh-baked bread and fried bacon all in one. Before you start wondering if this whole blog is going to end with me telling you how I've just killed my best friend along with everyone at her party, you should know that Mum's spent the last five years doing blood-desensitisation on me, and I wouldn't have come here at all if I'd thought I'd be a risk. But this is the first time I've ever truly been put to the test. Thankfully, having her scent to home in on stops me thinking about all the others that are floating up from the rooms below.

"I honestly had no idea it was going to happen," she apologised, yet again. "I told Jamie that you were coming, and he obviously saw how I excited I was. We'd talked about having an engagement party at some point, but I really didn't know he was planning this. It was a complete surprise. They shouldn't be here that much longer. Can I get you anything? There's cake, but I guess you don't eat that. Glen said you brought extra … you know …"

"Blood?"

"Right."

It takes an awesome type of person to be okay with you drinking blood in their spare room. But Lovisa is awesome.

"I'm fine. Honestly, I'm having fun listening in on all the conversations."

I didn't think it was appropriate to mention I'd used the time to start my own blog.

"For example, did you know that Jess and Lucy have been secretly dating for over two months?"

"What? No way? But now you mention it!"

Her smile flared and then faltered. All those years away from each other, and I can still read her like a book. I'll admit, that's a good feeling, even if her expression was telling me that she really needed to be playing the part of perfect host.

"It's OK. You go. I'll be fine. Though if you have a phone charger, that would be great."

"Give me one minute. There's one in my bedroom. And as soon as I get rid of these people, we can talk. I really am sorry, I never—"

"Lovisa, it's fine. Enjoy your surprise party."

She gave me another brief hug, fetched the charger then disappeared back downstairs. I have to give it to her; she is one brave girl. If I'd seen someone do what I did that night five years ago, I'm not sure I would have even let me in the house, let alone trusted me to be around her friends. But Lovisa's awesome. (I mentioned that, right?) Unfortunately, I've now got myself thinking about that night, and it seems only fair that I tell you since I brought it up.

If you've ever been heartbroken, you'll know what I mean when I say I was a wreck. Being forced to leave Fin felt like my ribs had been smashed into a thousand splintery shards, and every breath I took sent one of them ricocheting into my heart. I couldn't think straight. It just wasn't possible. Every thought I had was about him: what he was doing, who he was with, how often he thought of me, how he could have done this to me. I spent hours reliving our last kiss. Remembering where we were, and how long it had lasted and who had broken away first. I could almost feel the pressure of his soft lips against mine, the slight pleasure/pain as he bit my lower lip, the feel of his tongue exploring my mouth. It was actual insanity. I could never have believed that he would abandon me. Never in a million years. I mean, I would have scoured the earth to find him if his family just packed up one night and left with nothing more than some bullshit excuse about him being sick. That's what you do when you love someone, isn't it? You fight for them. But nope. Nothing.

Almost a year and a half after I turned, I was on the phone to Lovisa saying this exact same thing—for probably the seven-thousandth time.

"Why don't you just ask him?" she said.

"I told you. I can't. When I've tried to ring his house phone it says it's disconnected. The number must have changed."

"I think I saw him," she said, after a moment. "I drove past his house the other day. His mum is still there. He was outside, talking to her. It was either him or his little brother, the one you used to play in the band with. What was his name?"

"Noah," I replied.

"That's it. Well, they were all still at the house, so they haven't moved."

"Great."

The fact that she could see him but I couldn't felt like a heavy weight pushing down on my chest.

"That's not exactly useful to me, stuck here," I said.

"Why don't I come and get you? We'll put an end to all of this for good."

It wasn't the first time she had suggested meeting up, but before this, I had still been too wary. I wasn't exactly an experienced vampire. I usually had control around my family, but tranquillisings were still an almost fortnightly occurrence, and I wasn't sure what I was capable of. But I was antsy and frustrated and tired of every second of the day being consumed with thoughts about what could have been. So, unlike every other time that Lovisa had made this suggestion and I had dismissed her idea with a groan, this time I didn't.

"How?" I said, after a pause. "It's a three-hour drive, and I don't have a car, remember?"

"But I do."

"Well, there's the small issue of my parents. They're not just going to let me leave, only ..." A thought triggered at the back of my mind, and I raced downstairs to check the calendar on the fridge. "Mum has got a conference next month before she goes back to work full time. She's away for the whole weekend."

I could sense Lovisa smiling on the other end of the line.

"It looks like we're starting to form a plan," she said.

The next two weeks were spent plotting. Lovisa was at university and had been given a brand-new four-wheel drive for her eighteenth birthday by her parents, so she was fine. It was just my situation that needed sorting.

With Mum sorted, the next issue was Glen, who was now nearly fourteen and—as previously discussed—annoying with it. (Back then he wasn't in on any of it, and I just couldn't take the risk of him mucking things up.)

"Can't you send him on a sleepover that weekend?" I said to my parents over breakfast the next morning.

Lovisa and I had talked until the early hours about how awesome our reunion was going to be, which was fine for me as I don't need sleep, but I felt guilty about how knackered she was going to be for her lectures.

"He drives me mad when you're not here. He's always in my room, fiddling with the curtains and letting in light."

"That's so not true," he piped up.

"Is too," I countered.

I could see Mum mulling the idea over. She hated the idea of leaving me, and as much as she trusted Dad, he'd fallen into a research hole recently, which meant his focus on anything else was variable at best.

"Imagine if I got burned and accidentally lashed out at him by mistake," I added.

"It's probably not a bad idea," Mum conceded at last, concerned by the fighting that had already started. "I'll speak to Jamie's mum, see if you can spend the weekend there, instead."

"Can I take my iPad? Jamie's mum won't let him have one."

"We'll see," she replied.

Suppressing a grin, I finished my blood and headed back upstairs to message Lovisa. *Stage one sorted*, I sent.

Now all we had to do was deal with Dad. There was no point trying to get rid of him until Mum was well and truly out of the way. Any sniff of me being on my own and she would have had the plane turned around. I honestly believe she has the power to do that.

Friday finally arrived and off she went with a small suitcase, leaving a long list of instructions on the fridge. The moment she texted to say she was at the airport, I phoned Lovisa.

"Where are you?" I asked.

"I'm about fifteen minutes away."

"Okay, it's time. We need to do this."

"Are you all right, love?" Dad asked, appearing in the kitchen for a rare coffee break.

I discreetly hung up the phone.

"You look agitated."

"Just waiting for dinner time," I replied, then flicked

out my fangs just for fun. That joke never gets old. Even now it makes him jump. He offered a happy nod then switched on the kettle.

Two seconds later and the house phone rang. Given that no one ever uses it to speak to me, I let Dad get it and slipped upstairs to my room where I used my super hearing to listen in, already knowing the exact script she was going to use.

"Hello?" he said.

"Hello. Is that Professor David Colt?"

Now I could tell that it was Lovisa putting on a posh accent, and I'm fairly sure Mum and possibly even Glen would have known it was her, but my dad? He didn't have a clue. Considering how long Lovisa and I had been friends, it was actually kind of embarrassing how oblivious he was.

"Speaking, speaking. Yes, this is he. How can I help you?"

"Oh, Professor Colt, it's Professor Jean Kirkman here from Cambridge University."

Another distinct advantage when trying to trick my dad is that he's terrible with names. You could say it was Brad Pitt calling and he'd still spend ten minutes trying to figure out where he'd heard the name before.

"I'm so glad I got hold of you," she continued in her fake voice. "We've got a bit of an incident here. We have some specialists in the field who are convinced they are looking at evidence of recent lycanthrope activity."

"Lycanthrope you say?" he replied, his voice hitching higher.

(Lycanthrope is just a posh name for werewolf, in case you didn't know, but she couldn't say that. Even my dad would have smelt something fishy. Scientists hate using words that other people know the meaning of. It's a superiority thing. You need to speak their lingo if you want them to take you seriously.)

"Yes," Lovisa continued. "They're there right now. I know it's a massive ask, but we are desperate for a second opinion and your name was at the top of our list. Naturally, if these findings bear fruit, you would be credited in any papers."

A pause followed. I could almost hear the cogs whirring in my dad's head.

"Cambridge you say?"

"I know it's awfully last minute. If you can't make it, I'm sure I can—"

"No, no, no. Give me a second. Can I call you back, Professor …?"

"Kirkman. Of course. Let me give you my direct number," she said, straying from the script a little, but as smooth as anything as she did. A moment later, Dad was standing outside my door. He cleared his throat before knocking once.

"Come in," I said, lying on my bed, trying to look as calm and bored as possible.

The door creaked open, and his head peeked around the corner.

"Ah, you're here," he said.

"Were you expecting me to be somewhere else?" I replied.

He moved from one side of the room to the other before coming to a stop back beside my bed.

"Is everything all right, Dad?" I asked, trying to maintain the relaxed pose and natural voice, despite the fact that the next five minutes would require the best acting of my entire life. "Is Mum OK?"

"Oh yes, yes," he said, and the pacing starting again. "I just wondered what you were up to this weekend. This evening, really. Whether you had any plans?"

"Plans?" I said. "Well, you know, I thought I might head into the city. I hear there are some great raves going on."

"Raves?"

"Yeah, you know. Loads of young kids who'd be too drunk to notice if I feed off them."

Dad's eyes bulged. Seriously, he is the easiest man on the planet to wind up. It would be amusing if it wasn't so … scrap that. It's always amusing. (I don't want you guys to get the wrong impression here. I've mentioned about him being useless a fair bit and dragging us on holidays we really didn't want to go on, or spending days locked up in his study and now here he is contemplating abandoning his vampire daughter to go on some wild goose chase looking for werewolves, but really, he's not a bad dad. He's not. He just gets a little bit *hyper-focused,* as he calls it. Don't go feeling sorry for my mum in all of this, either. She knew what he was like when she married him. It was *why* she married him. Anyway, I feel like I should get that out there before you start judging him too harshly.)

"I'm joking, Dad," I said, realising it might not be a good idea to wind him up too much. "I was planning on resting. Not sure what's going on with me. I think maybe I over fed at lunch."

"Resting?"

"Pretty much. I feel a forty-eight-hour doze coming on. I thought I might watch the new Jennifer Lawrence film first if it's on Netflix now. Mum's stocked the fridge up, so yeah, I'm pretty much set. Unless there's something you wanted us to do together? You can join me for the film if you want?"

"Film? Together?" Cue another weird eye movement. "No, no. Not if you're all right. Not if you're happy," he said. He moved towards the door, paused and turned back. "You wouldn't mind if I pop out for a few hours, would you? I mean you're not going to need anything, are you? I might be gone a little while."

I shrugged, trying to look like I didn't care in the slightest what he did.

"I'm fine," I said.

"I could lock you in?"

"If you want?"

(Like that would stop me.)

"Great," he replied.

A moment later he's on the phone to the fake professor and then packing his briefcase.

Now all I had to do was wait.

Chapter 6

Date: March 2nd
Followers: 16
Time: 10:50 p.m.
Hours stuck in this room: 4.25
Number of drunk people in the flat: 27
Number of times Lovisa has apologised to me: 348
Number of times Glen has come to check on his vampire sister during this party: 1

I GUESS I should take it as a compliment that Glen doesn't feel the need to keep checking up on me. Then again, it's not very often he gets to let his hair down. It's fair to say he puts a tonne of pressure on himself. He's the high-flier. Captain of the rugby team, first violin in the orchestra, dating the captain of the cricket team, all while keeping his vampire sister a secret. And he's currently deciding whether to study medicine or aeronautical engineering at university.

For those of you who are nosey, yes, you do detect a slight twinge of jealously. There was a time, nearly a decade ago, when I wanted to head to university myself to study English literature, mainly so I could read all day. But balancing lectures and parties with an extreme intolerance to UV rays isn't something I fancy. Let's be honest, if I can't even trust myself to socialise with people for an event as important as my best friend's engagement party, then I'm hardly going to be able to manage a two-hundred-person lecture hall, am I?

Even weirder than the fact that Glen hasn't checked on me again, is that Mum and Dad haven't either. Not at all. Which considering how late it is, is not what I expected. Maybe they're staying in contact with Glen so they don't seem to be babying me all the time. To be honest, I have to say I think it's pretty reckless of them. It's like they don't remember I'm a blood-sucking monster.

Anyway, enough wallowing. I was telling you how I almost killed someone. Twenty minutes after Dad left, Lovisa pulled up outside the house. Given that it was not quite sunset, I had smothered myself in factor 100, but could still feel my skin prickling as I ran out to meet her.

"God, I've missed you," she said, putting her arms around me the second I was in the car.

Whether it was because it was Lovisa, or just another human, I don't know, but touching her sent a thousand tiny sparks of electricity shooting across my skin. I gasped, then breathed in her scent, trying to absorb everything I'd missed the previous 18 months. And I could smell it all. The things that had changed; the people she'd kissed, the countries she'd visited, the gardens she'd walked through. They were all there, trapped in her skin, a part of her.

"Are you sure about this?" I said, as she turned the key in the ignition and started the engine. "It's going to be a long drive. Just you and me."

"Of course I am. I drove all the way here didn't I?"

"Yes, but that's not quite the same, is it? And when we get there ..."

"It'll be fine. By my calculation, we'll arrive about eleven. Nice and dark. You can talk to Fin, take a midnight stroll or whatever, then when the sun comes up you can camp out at his house or my parents until tomorrow evening, and we'll head back."

"We could just cover the windows at the back of the car and I'll wrap myself up in a blanket there," I suggested. "I don't want to use up your whole weekend."

"Are you kidding? I want to be here."

I smiled gratefully but noticed her lips twisting with a slight look of concern.

"What about your dad?" she said. "What if he comes home early and finds out it's all been a ruse?"

I shook my head.

"He never comes back early from Cambridge. He knows too many people there."

It was true. Back when I was human, we used to go for an afternoon visit, then Mum, Glen and I would end up coming home without him while he'd stay up there for a week, talking to all his old uni friends about some ancient witch trials or something equally macabre.

"You're sure?"

"Positive."

"Good, because I made us a playlist."

Her eyes lingered on me, and I could tell she was trying to see it. The difference. The vampire.

"Have you got enough blood?" she asked.

"I'm good to go."

"And you're not ... hungry?"

"I'm good," I promised her again.

For the first couple of hours, Lovisa was amazingly chilled, if not more than a little excited to discuss the fact her best friend was a vampire.

"You could become a vigilante," she said. "Use your super strength to save people from burning buildings."

"Then feed off them afterwards," I added.

She briefly took her eyes off the road to frown at me.

"You could feed off of the bad guys, obviously."

"That makes more sense."

"Besides, I thought you said you don't have to eat all the time?"

"I don't. But that's rather like saying you don't have to eat a family-sized bucket of popcorn just because it's available."

"So you do want to eat people?"

"I wouldn't say *want to.*"

After that she began to get a little twitchy.

"You drank before you left, didn't you?" she said, for the fourth time.

"I did."

"And you brought extra?"

"Plenty. Trust me. I am not going feed on you. But, since you're worried."

I leaned forward and pulled something out of the small bag I had brought with me.

"Here, take this."

I checked the cap was secure before holding it out to her.

"What's that?"

"A tranquilliser autoinjector. Bit like an EpiPen. You did first aid—just jab it in my neck and it'll give you plenty of time to drive me back home and lock me in the house."

"You want me to drug you?"

"Only if you think you need to."

She took it from me, turned it over once and then placed it in the cupholder beside her.

"Okay," she said. "I'll keep it, but I don't want to use it."

"And I'd rather you didn't, trust me."

With the option of putting me into a comatose state, if necessary, Lovisa seemed to relax into the drive, and the rest of the journey went by in a flash. Talking on the phone was great, but having her there with me, laughing at my jokes and my epic vampire fails, it started to feel like old times again. It may sound strange, but every minute spent together in the car made me feel less and less like a freak and more like a human being. Unfortunately, it also made thoughts of Fin harder and harder to ignore.

"So you really haven't spoken to him?" I said. "Not at all?"

"Not since that time he came over and gave me a box of your stuff. He looked a mess then."

"But he didn't ask about me or if you knew where I was?"

"He didn't say anything, other than, 'Here you go.'"

She could obviously sense me starting to slip back into deep thoughts, so she brightened her voice and said, "I saw his little brother again, though."

"Noah? Did you speak to him?"

"No. It was at some gig. He was playing the bass. Though one of the girls I was with knew him. I think she said he'd gone off to art college."

I *ummed* and *ahhed* in response but didn't really care

all that much. Art college seemed about right for him, but I wanted to know about Fin. He was bound to have headed off to some great university. Probably to study English or philosophy or something like that, and now working some fancy job somewhere.

The conversation continued and she brought me up to speed on old school friends and family members, and we talked about films we'd watched and books we'd read. But in truth, my thoughts never really left Fin.

We turned off the motorway onto smaller roads, and little by little, the scenery became more familiar.

"Is that a new shopping centre?" I asked, as a building so enormous it looked like it was straight out of an American teen film appeared.

Lovisa glanced over her shoulder.

"Yes. It's been there a year or so. It's okay."

"And what happened to the cinema?" I asked, as we passed a roundabout I was certain I knew.

"Oh, that relocated about six months ago. They've got an IMAX at the new one. I saw one of Spiderman movies there. It was amazing. Maybe we could go together sometime?"

"Maybe."

I hummed, my gaze lost outside the window. My nerves were beginning to rise, shudders running down my spine. My senses had been on overdrive since smelling Lovisa. They had been easy to deal with when we were on the motorway. Petrol fumes and newly laid tarmac were pretty much it, but since entering the towns, there had been so much more. Restaurants, rubbish and people. So many people all around me and the smell of sweat, tears and blood, so distinct I could almost taste it. I closed my eyes and tried to drown myself in my friend's aroma. Somehow she was a safe zone. Something I knew I couldn't hurt. The steady rhythm of her heartbeat became my focus.

"The family who live there now have six children," she said, her words breaking my concentration. "Can you believe it? Six. Crazy, right?"

"Sorry, what?"

That's when I looked up and gulped.

"My old home."

The first time I'd kissed Fin had been in that house. The first time he told me he loved me. The first time I fell asleep in his arms while we watched TV together and the first time I had let his hands explore my body. That was when it sank in why we were there. This wasn't just some silly old trip down memory lane. I wasn't your average teenager on a catch up with their long-lost best friend. I was going to see Fin. I was going to get answers. I was going to hear from his own mouth how he could have given me up, let me leave without even trying to see me first. I was going to learn why he broke my heart.

I had spent a substantial amount of time during the journey, and before, considering my arrival at his house. Ringing the doorbell late at night when his family were asleep wouldn't go well. Besides, the more people I came into contact with, the more pressure I was putting myself under. Fortunately, I had a plan.

This bit is going to sound cheesy, I'm afraid, but I can't help it. We were teenagers in love, and we adhered to far too many clichés. Back then, we thought we were adventurous and wild and original. We were really just an average episode of Dawson's Creek. (Go retro guys; you won't regret it.) Fin lived in a small, detached house with his mum, gran and Noah. He shared a bedroom with his brother, meaning there was never any privacy. Fortunately, their room was above the kitchen extension and there was a large flat roof outside the window. It was easy enough to climb out onto it, and we would sit up there in the evenings reading our books while Noah sat inside drawing on his sketch pad. (Funny how I remember that now.) We would take blankets and snacks with us, and that little space became our own private world. All I could think about was that rooftop and Fin's arms wrapped around me. I barely noticed that Lovisa had brought the car to a stop just around the corner from his house.

"Do you want me to come with you?" she asked, cutting the engine.

Somewhere in the distance, motorbikes engines were being revved, TVs blared in living rooms, teenagers were shouting over at the park. Taking a deep breath, I tried to block it all out.

"No," I said. "I need to do this alone."

My nerves were through the roof, but I let the steadying scent of Lovisa calm me as much as it could. I may not need air, but several deep breaths followed before I opened the passenger door and closed it behind me as silently as I could, then offered her a wave. She smiled encouragingly, crossing her fingers and raising them to the windscreen. A second later, I was over the fence and into Fin's backyard. Adrenaline rushed through me as I climbed the drainpipe onto the flat roof. Climbing wasn't something I'd practiced since becoming a vampire, but clearly it was a newfound talent. Honestly, I had no upper body strength as a human. Monkey bars were a serious no go for me back then, and don't even get me started on pull ups. But I was up onto the roof like I was born to do it, and guess what? The window was shut.

Now you know how in all those US shows the kids' bedrooms have those windows that slide up from the outside so the girl can sneak into guy's bedroom and the parents never know? Well, we don't have those in the UK. Here we have ones that unlatch on the inside, open outwards and are physically impossible to budge from the outside. Impossible to do quietly, at least.

So I was stuck. I could either use my vampire strength and rip the window clean away from the wall or knock loud enough to wake Fin up and have him open it. Clearly, the second was a better option, but the only thing was, he wasn't alone. Even through the glass and with the curtains closed, I could hear two heart beats drumming away, two people breathing and two lots of blood pumping around their bodies, which meant there was a good chance I would wake his little brother, too. It took only a couple of seconds for me to decide I didn't have a choice. If I wanted to see him, I was just going to have to take the risk. I began tapping gently on the glass.

At first no one heard, so I tried a little harder and after a few stronger raps, noticed a change in the sounds. One of the heartbeats had quickened a little and the breathing staggered. Straining to hear as this person pushed back the bedclothes and dropped onto the ground, my anxiety skyrocketed. The sound of footsteps reverberated through the floorboards, and I had to stop myself yelling with happiness when I saw a shadow flickering behind the curtains. I was certain it was him. The smell of his deodorant, his skin. The room was filled with it. Something close to a sob rose in my throat as I thought of all the things I was going to say to him. All the things he'd be able to tell me. I was picturing his face and the way he would hold me and kiss me when the curtain suddenly whipped back.

For a split second, I thought I was seeing my reflection: mousey hair, grey eyes, a confused expression. But then it shifted and the strap of her bra slipped over her shoulder. Then I looked beyond her. Lying next to her dent in the mattress was a body I recognised, with his dark skin, thick hair and the sharp curve of his shoulder blades. Everything that my fingers yearned to reach out and touch. My throat tightened even more as my eyes moved back to the girl, then to Fin on the bed, then back to the girl again. She was dressed only in her underwear, a butterfly tattoo creeping down the side of her arm. Nausea filled me. She had been in bed with him. Sleeping with him. His arm over hers, skin touching skin, near enough naked. I was still frozen, staring at the blue-green pattern of the butterfly wings, when her mouth opened and a scream shot from her mouth.

That was when my fangs came out.

I was a wreck, and you can't blame me. I had gone in search of the love of my life, only to find him in bed with another girl. Okay, it had been two years since I'd seen him, and yes, from what my mother had said, he probably thought I was as good as dead to him, but come on, would a little bit of grieving have been too much to ask for? After all, we'd been together for two years, although we hadn't made the overnight leap yet, but there he'd been, lying next to her in his home like it was the most natural thing in the world. Then someone switched on a light.

The light. Now I was screaming. My senses were on overload. Fin was awake and I knew within seconds he'd be on his feet by the window. So without giving myself time to think, I did the only thing I could. I jumped off the roof and ran back around the corner towards the car. Lovisa was still in the driver's seat, headphones on listening to her music, and I was about to open the door and stick a needle in myself, when a man stepped out in front of me.

With everything going on, I hadn't even thought to listen out for anyone else out on the street. Waves of alcohol billowed from his pores, but even that didn't distract from the aroma of his blood. Maybe he'd cut himself somewhere; I can't say. All I knew was once my senses had locked onto it, there was no going back. The blood lust was real. Real and overwhelming. Walking forwards, I blocked his path, causing him to start and drop the bottle he was carrying. It shattered into a wet mess around our feet.

"What the fuck?" he slurred.

He pointed a finger at me, and I knocked his arm away. I know it must have hurt, because I've seen the expression Glen sometimes makes when I think I've just casually pushed him aside. But he was too drunk to dwell on it. His lost beer was definitely his biggest concern.

"Bitch! You owe me a drink!"

A car drove up the road behind him, the headlights glaring straight at me, but even that wasn't enough to distract me from what I wanted. I edged forwards, forcing him back until he was pressed against Lovisa's car door, trapping her and the tranquilliser inside.

"Funnily enough, I was thinking the exact same thing," I replied.

"What the hell?"

His face paled as he clocked my fangs.

"I think you need to work on your manners. You never know who you might be calling a bitch."

"I … I …"

His skin was white now. His eyes darted from side to side as he desperately searched for a way out. But there was none. I had him.

"The venom will stop this from hurting too much," I said, unable to stop an insane grin spreading across my face. "I promise, I won't take much."

And just like that, I sank my teeth into his neck.

Dark right? I bet for a moment there you were thinking I wouldn't go through with it. But there's a reason why I've been terrified to leave the house for the last five years. And it isn't just that I fed on some random stranger. It's because I loved it. Even now, I can remember how it felt as the blood pulsed from his artery and the way the thick liquid filled my mouth as I hurried to gulp down every drop. It felt as if every cell in my body was exploding, making me feel alive in a way I hadn't experienced since I was, well, alive. The strength, the power. The euphoria drove me on.

Now, I look back on it with repulsion. I think it's what any ex-addict must feel, realising how much their habit screwed them up yet at the same time was the only thing holding them together. Every mouthful made me want another, even as Lovisa scrambled out of the passenger door and started screaming at me, her hands shaking so much she dropped the syringe on the ground.

So what made me stop? Why didn't I drain him until there was nothing left? It wasn't willpower, I can tell you that much. Those headlights I mentioned earlier. Turns out they didn't belong to some random passing car. When my mother got to the airport, she discovered she'd forgotten her passport. First trip away in nearly two years and a blood-drinking daughter to worry about and she'd forgotten to go through her checklist properly. Halfway home she rang Dad who told her he was out hunting werewolves. When there was no answer from the house phone when she called, she hazarded a guess as to where I'd gone (probably complaining about not seeing Fin for a year and half was a bit of a giveaway). Bounding out of her car, she scooped up the syringe and jabbed me straight in the neck. Catching me in her arms as my body succumbed to the sedative, she turned to Lovisa.

"Open the back door!" she ordered.

Lovisa did as she was told and Mum bundled me across the seat.

"What about him?" Lovisa asked gesturing to the drunk bleeding all over the road.

"I'll get him to hospital. Now just get her out of here."

And then my consciousness also succumbed.

After that, it took a couple of months before I'd even come out of my room. I would wake up every two or three days, drink barely a mouthful, then give myself another shot to knock myself out again.

I know that guy was fine. Mum said they did a blood transfusion as soon as she took him in. She went back a couple of days later, by which point he'd already been discharged, apparently with the intention of heading to the nearest pub to celebrate. That was one fortunate thing about my choice of victim. No matter how loud he screamed *vampire*, no one would believe him. But it's what could have happened that scared me so much. The way I lost control. The way I wanted to lose control. I'll never risk feeding directly from another human again. Not if my life – Shit.

Shit. Shit. Shit.

Guys I'm really sorry, I have to go. Something's happened.

This can't be real. It can't …

Oh my God, what the hell am I going to do?

He's here.

Fin is downstairs.

Chapter 7

Date: March 3rd
Followers: 36
Time: 2 a.m.

OKAY THE GOOD news is all the guests have finally gone, and Lovisa has persuaded Jamie to stay at a mate's house so we don't have to worry about him being here, too. The plan was to drive back tonight, but Glen is in no fit state. I guess if we'd been really desperate I could have driven—I had lessons and everything even though I didn't pass—but his car is a nightmare. It's so freaking old and temperamental only he can drive it. Mum and Dad want to hold off buying him a new one until he goes to university. They want to get him one as a surprise. And I know it's a nice idea, but I don't think this one is going to last until then.

Anyway, back to the current situation.

Part of me feels like I should have been listening in better, paying attention to how much he'd had to drink, but he was having such a good night. Thankfully, he's a gentle drunk. If he became a blabber mouth we would really be screwed. But now there's only him, Lovisa and me in the flat and he's decided that he has to stay up until I go to sleep. Trust me, there's no point trying to reason with him when he gets like this. So as soon as I've finished updating you I'm going to let him give me a small dose of tranquilliser, so he doesn't have to be on drunken high alert all night. It might help settle me a bit too. And believe me when I say I need something to do that. I honestly I can't believe it. I seriously can't.

As you already know, I was typing away, chatting to you guys when I freaked out. The front door had been opening and closing all night as Lovisa and Jamie's friends filtered in and out while I'd stayed out of the way, keeping it all under control. But this time a scent threaded up the stairs, and when it reached me I swear my heart did a full somersault.

I don't remember actively smelling Fin when I was human. I couldn't tell you what he smelt of, other than deodorant and general muskiness, but there was something so intense about the odour that hit me when that front door opened that my memory exploded, with hundreds of tiny moments flashing through my mind. Him kissing his way down my neck, while his fingertips run up and down my thigh edging ever closer.

I dropped to the ground and crawled on the floor, looking for my bag and the six tranquilliser shots I'd packed just in case. I wanted to sedate myself. I needed to block him out, because otherwise I was going to lose control again. But as I readied the needle in my hand, I couldn't do it. I just couldn't. I needed to see him. Not even to speak to him. Just see him. To know I wasn't losing my mind. With my hand trembling, I opened the bedroom door for the first time all evening and walked to the top of the stairs leading to the ground floor of the apartment. That's when I saw him. Standing at the bottom of the staircase like we were in some freaking Cinderella rewrite.

We must have both looked like we'd seen a ghost which, technically, he kind of had. I could hear his heart pounding and his breath quickening as he took the stairs two at a time to reach me.

"Fin," I whispered.

For a moment, we just stood there. Me staring up at him. Him gazing down at me. And in that split second, I realised my mistake. I'd never had to look *up* at Fin like that. He was taller than me, but not loads. So unless he'd grown another five inches, which didn't seem likely, I realised it wasn't my long lost love at all.

"Actually it's—"

"Noah," I finished for him, still breathless from the shock of it all. "I'm sorry, just you look so … wow … I had no idea … wow … just wow."

"I get it," he grinned. "Wow."

I was speechless, for so many reasons. Firstly, because for a moment there I thought I was standing in front of the love of my life, my ex-boyfriend who I hadn't seen in over half a decade. But the reason for the *wow*, was because I was looking at his baby brother. And his baby brother had grown up.

It's not unreasonable that I'd mistake Noah for Fin: same shaped eyes, same chin, same hair. At the same time there were some fairly obvious differences, too. There were the tattoos that I could see through the thin fabric of his shirt. (Fin did not care for tattoos one bit). And there was the playful smile Noah was wearing, very different to Fin who didn't have a natural smile. It was always a little forced even when it was genuine.

"I didn't know you and Lovisa were still in touch," I said. "She didn't mention it."

"We're not. It was Jamie who invited me. I did some work up at his office a few weeks ago and we got on great. So here I am."

"Work?"

"I paint. Murals mostly but anything that needs painting, really. He invited me. I didn't even realise that his fiancée was our Lovisa until I got here."

He bit down on his lip and studied me. I wasn't sure if I wanted to curl in on myself or stand up straight so he could see me better. One second of silence turned into two, then three and I was starting to wonder if I should just leave, when he spoke again. This time quieter. More considered.

"How are you? You got sick again, didn't you? Fin never really spoke about it. He was pretty cut up."

"He wasn't the only one," I replied.

He nodded, thoughtfully.

"But you're better now?"

I pressed my lips together and shook my head. Another silence was swelling around us, and I wasn't sure which way it was going to go. Noah looked downstairs where the girl he'd obviously arrived with was waiting for him.

"You go," I said. "It was nice to see you again."

It was his turn to shake his head. "It's fine, she could make friends in a morgue."

He laughed at his own joke.

"Honestly, if anything I hold her back."

I looked down and sure enough she already had a drink in her hand and was deep in animated conversation with some of Lovisa's work friends. I turned back to Noah. His eyes were still on me and so intense it felt like I had stumbled out into a sunny day.

"Let's go down and get you a drink?" he said. "We can catch up properly."

"Actually," I replied, "would you mind just talking up here instead? I'm not really up for the whole people thing."

The first few minutes after I asked Noah to stay were pretty freaking awkward. We had gone back into the spare bedroom and were sat at opposite ends of the double bed, looking anywhere but at each other. At my request, we'd kept the lights off although the city still glittered below us through the open windows. Light bulbs don't cause the same photosensitive reaction that sunlight does. I can cope just fine. But I can also see perfectly in the dark (another vampire perk), and it makes it easy to spot if someone is lying to me. All those little eye twitches. Those taps of the fingers and scratches at the cheek that they don't know I'm aware of. I noticed those little lying signs all the time when I first changed and asked Mum about Fin. She'd scratch her temple when she said he was doing fine. Or her nostrils would flare when she said she didn't know why his phone wouldn't ring.

Like I said, we didn't speak to start with, but Noah's heartbeat was going crazy, and his breathing was abnormally shallow and fast. He almost seemed afraid, but there was no way he could know I was a vampire.

"So, the light," he said eventually. "That's part of the problem? You can't go out in it? Is that it?"

"Yeah, it's part of it. Photosensitivity," I said. "It's the main thing, I guess."

Other than drinking blood, I could have added, but I didn't think he'd want to hear that bit.

"It seriously weakens my immune system."

"Sounds tough."

"It's not been easy," I admitted.

His heart was still pounding as he looked over to where I was sitting. I tried to read his expression, but there was too much in there. So, instead, I just watched him and felt the silence building around us again. I finally cut it short with the first thing that came to mind.

"How's your gran?" I asked. "Is she doing any better? She must be in her eighties now."

"She died," he replied. "Six years ago. Not long after you left."

My stomach dropped.

"I'm sorry," I said. "She was a lovely woman."

"She was. Liked you a lot, too, from what I remember. It was a tough time, for all of us."

I smiled sadly, even though he couldn't see it.

"What about you?" I said, trying to bring a more positive tone to the conversation. "What have you been up to?"

I could tell right away that he wasn't going to answer my question. His jaw locked and for a second I thought he might walk out. Instead, he clenched and unclenched his fists before he finally spoke.

"He was a mess," he said. "When you left, he was a total wreck. I'd never seen him like that. None of us had. We didn't know what we were meant to do."

"I didn't have a choice," I said. "I was sick. Seriously sick. My parents took me away. You think I wanted to leave him?"

"He wouldn't have cared. He'd have stood by you. You know that. He would have moved heaven and earth for you."

"I didn't have a choice," I repeated. "My parents wouldn't let me say goodbye."

Whether he could tell or not, Noah was looking straight at me. His lips were closed, and he hummed audibly as he contemplated what I was telling him. I was trying to decide if it meant that he believed me or not, when he gave me the answer, although not the one I'd been hoping for.

"I'm gonna be honest," he said. "I don't buy it."

"You don't?"

"No, I don't."

Now, to have someone look you in the eye (sort of), and tell you that they think you're lying, even when you are lying (sort of), is not a good feeling.

"You want to see?" I said, my voice ripe with indignation. "Go on then, find a UV light. Or we can wait until morning. See what happens to me then if I go outside."

"No." He waved my comment away. "That's not what I don't believe. I get you're not well. I just don't get how you could treat someone like that if you really loved them? I just don't think you could. Really have loved him, that is."

It was a sharp jab, and maybe I imagined it, but I swear my fangs tingled.

"You think I didn't love him?"

"I dunno," he said. "I mean, you're okay now, right? You're fine to come visiting Lovisa. Attend her party."

"Attend her party? Has it escaped your notice that I've shut myself up in a room here on my own? I haven't left my home in years. I haven't seen any one in *years*. This is it. You're witnessing me on my first outing *ever* since I got sick. Do you have any idea how difficult this was to do? I didn't even want to come."

"Then why did you?"

"You wouldn't understand."

"Well make me, because right now it seems like coming to Lovisa's party takes priority over the guy you supposedly loved."

"It was a long time ago, Noah."

"It was seven years. I keep count."

Another silence fell between us as I bit down on my tongue. His heart was going like a hammer, wielded by someone who was angry, which only made me even madder. A large part of me wanted to walk out, there and then, but all that awaited me outside this room were drunk strangers and a brother who was getting to let his hair down for the first time in ages.

"Surely you could have come and seen us? Seen him?" Noah said with a sigh. "Just a phone call or something … anything."

"I tried to. I—"

"Would it really have been that hard?"

"You don't understand, I—"

"I had to watch my big brother mourning. And you weren't even dead."

"Wasn't I? It sure as hell felt like it."

It was the first thing I'd said that stopped him talking, and now I'd got the floor I had no intention of giving it up. "I felt like I had died," I said, trying to get my words out before my voice broke. "Leaving Fin, leaving my life, leaving everything I loved and not having a choice in the matter, it felt like I had died. Is that at least some consolation to you? Does that make you feel a little better?"

A palpable tension filled the air between us.

"Not particularly," he replied, before letting out a sigh. "You took years from him. From us. You know that? He moved away after Gran died. He said he needed a change, but we all knew he was still grieving for you."

My anger softened a fraction.

"I didn't know that. How would I?"

"He cut all contact. Even with me. He was my best friend, and you stole him from me."

"Noah …" I reached out my hand towards him but pulled it back before I got too close.

"Three years he was gone, without a word. My big

brother missed my eighteenth birthday. Can you imagine? Fin, missing something like that? In one year, I lost you, I lost my brother, and I lost my gran. Have you any idea what that was like? And do you know what it was like for my mum?"

Lots of so-called authorities will tell you that vampires don't cry or that they cry blood or black tears or some other nonsense. It's not true. We can cry, but to do so means ripping all the moisture from within us. And we have a serious lack of that. (It's not just because we barely drink. The fact that we don't need oxygen or food is because we don't respire, and respiration releases water into the body. Look it up in a science textbook if you don't believe me.) Anyway, crying is like ripping the life out of every single cell of our body. It hurts like you couldn't possibly imagine. But at that precise moment, as I sat on the bed with Noah, everything was already hurting so much that it didn't seem to matter.

"A letter, a call, that's all it would have taken. You could have brought him back to us."

"I am so sorry. I didn't realise ..."

Through the tears, a thought struck me, but Noah was already standing.

"I'm glad you're feeling well enough to get out," he said. "You'll understand if I don't mention that I've seen you to anyone."

He stepped across to the door and reached for the handle, but I was up in an instant and grabbed his arm.

"Wait."

He hesitated. My foot tapped anxiously, certain he was going to leave, but then he turned around to me in the dark. We were standing so close that I could feel his breath on my face and the static buzz that rose from his skin.

"What?" he said. "What is it you want, Merrewyn?"

I paused.

"He went away, you said, the year I left. And he was gone for three years?

"Yeah, he left the day after Gran's funeral, just packed a bag and went. Said he'd call when he'd settled down a bit. And when he came back all those years later, it was an even bigger shit show that I really don't want to get into right now."

I shook my head, trying to get rid of the thought at the back of my mind, but it wouldn't let go. After a moment, I realised I had no choice but to air it.

"And he didn't come back once. Didn't stay at yours?"

"You're kidding, right?" His voice was laced with bitterness. "One postcard every four months. That's what I got. Half of them weren't even in his handwriting."

"But that makes no sense. He can't have been gone then. He can't have."

"Trust me, he was. I know. I was the one at home, picking up Mum after everything else."

I ran my tongue across my lips, trying to decide what

to say. Fin used to have this annoying habit of knowing when something was on my mind. *Just spit it out,* he would say. His brother, it appeared, had inherited the same quality.

"What?" he said. "What are you not telling me?"

Chapter 8

Date: March 3rd
Followers: 55

GIVEN how calm and chilled this morning started out, I can't believe it's finishing like this, with me pacing up and down a hospital corridor. And there's nothing I can do. Literally nothing.

The smell of blood is everywhere. Absolutely everywhere. But I can't leave. Not while Mum needs me. And Dad ... Shit, Dad ... Why do I have the sinking feeling in my gut that all this is somehow my fault? Call it vampire intuition or whatever, but somehow I know. It is.

Chapter 9

Date: March 4th
Followers: 64

THANK you so much for your messages of concern. They're really appreciated. And for those of you worried about Glen, he's fine. It's my dad that's sick. You know how I mentioned it was strange that I hadn't heard from my parents all last night? Yeah, well now I know the reason why.

And what's so fucking frustrating is that yesterday morning I was actually feeling good about life (afterlife). Like maybe there was going to be more to my existence than cat videos and Netflix. But, yet again, I'm faced with the truth. I ruin lives.

Yesterday morning started out great. Really great. It was odd having breakfast in someone else's house after seven years of seeing the same rank kitchen counter, sink and fridge every single day. Like I said before, I can't really blame my parents for the state of the place. They would have people in to fix things up. I'm the problem.

The night of the party though …

That night, although I was hardly *out-there*, finally made me feel like I might be able to join the real world again. Like maybe my parents having a new kitchen might actually be doable.

Admittedly the only people I spoke to were Glen, Lovisa and Noah, but I had been in the same building as nearly thirty people. Thirty. That's the same as a whole class when I was at school or a really small cinema showing. Anyway, there's no way that can happen now. To be honest, I don't know what's going to happen at all.

But I'm getting ahead of myself; I need to catch you up with what's been going on. So let's jump back to yesterday morning.

"So, are you going to tell me what you and Noah talked about?" Lovisa asked as she dropped a plate of croissants in front of Glen while eyeing me with an undisguised look of glee.

I was busy smothering myself in SPF 100 in case she fancied raising the blackout blinds a little, although she kept insisting she was fine keeping them down. Honestly, a place like this would be a death trap for a vampire if the power failed. I'd feel it necessary to get good old-fashioned curtains as a backup, just in case.

"You two were alone in the bedroom for a long time," she continued. "Is there anything you want to mention?"

"Noah was looking pretty hot," Glen added as he sipped on a black coffee.

"Please don't tell me you're insinuating what I think you are?" I said, offering them both my most scathing glower. "I'm a twenty-four-year-old vampire virgin, remember?"

"Technically you're a seventeen-year-old vampire virgin," Glen said, reaching across and grabbing a croissant.

"You know I could break every single bone in your body without even breaking into a sweat?" I replied.

"I do, but it doesn't change the fact that you're technically only seventeen. Anyway, are you going to fill us in or not?."

Like I said, at this point in the day I was feeling good. I might even go so far as to say excited. Not about Noah, just about how smoothly the whole night had gone with no disasters. And I knew that Lovisa and Glen were curious about Noah. Just like you lot.

As I said in my last post, Fin had that annoying habit of knowing when I was hiding something, and Noah had the exact same skill.

"What is it?" he said. "What are you not telling me?"

I tried to decide what to say but couldn't find the right words so just used whatever ones became available as I spoke.

"I did come back to see him. It was a while after I left. A year and a half, actually."

"What?"

"I had to sneak out of the house. Lovisa came and got me."

"You came back?"

He fumbled and turned on the light by the door. I nodded quickly, aware of just how intense his eyes were on me.

"My parents didn't know. They would never have allowed it. The risks back then were ... Anyway, he was in his room. I saw him through the window. And there was another girl sharing his bed. I couldn't stay. I couldn't speak to him. He'd moved on and I knew that was what I had to do, too."

Noah remained exactly where he was. Frozen, barely blinking, looking straight at me.

"The girl," he said, eventually. "Did she have a tattoo across her shoulder? A butterfly—"

"A purple one, it stretched all the way down here."

I traced a line down from the top of my shoulder.

"That wasn't Fin," he said. "That was me."

I shook my head and laughed. "I have pretty good eyesight."

"Apparently not. Believe me. Fin had left by then. It was me."

"I just thought that he …"

Another second passed and he dropped his head and groaned.

"Holy crap. I thought she was nuts, seriously unhinged. Well, she was a bit nuts, who gets butterfly tattoos nowadays? But she kept screaming about a girl with glowing eyes staring at her through the window. So there really was a girl."

"There really was."

"I guess the glowing-eyes part was a bit of an exaggeration."

A cough caught in my throat. The truth is, very occasionally, in highly stressful situations my eyes have been known to emit a slight luminosity. But that wasn't something I planned on saying. "It must have been a bit of a shock," I said instead.

An amused chuckled drifted from Noah's lips.

"That's one way of putting it. Man, you have no idea how much trouble you got me in. Mum didn't know I was sneaking girls into my room at night. She was furious. I thought she was going to kick me out. I had to grovel like you wouldn't believe. And obviously I never saw the girl again. I thought she was a crazy."

He stopped talking, and I thought that maybe he was still mad about the whole thing, when he suddenly started laughing. Full on laughing. And he had an amazingly cute laugh. Nothing like Fin at all. Far lower. And freer. Then, without knowing why, I found myself laughing, too.

"What is it about you?" he said, quietly.

I thought he'd leave at that point, and he did, but not until he'd asked for my number. I'm not sure now whether I did the right thing, giving him a fake one, but I did. What on earth could we even talk about? How much I loved his brother? How I still think about him? How I'm currently in need of blood donors if he fancies signing up. No, it was a chance meeting. That was it, and now it's done with. So, there you go. The end of the story.

Also, Lovisa was really cool about the blood situation.

"I could come up to yours if you like? If that's easier for you?" she offered. "We could make it a girls' night. Watch a film, a bottle of red each. Get it. *Bottle of red?*"

"That sounds great."

"I think you should come here," Glen said. "You managed great last night. I think it was good for you."

"I shut myself in a darkened room for five hours," I reminded him.

Obviously, we have different ideas as to what constitutes doing great.

"Yes, but with dozens of people in the same house as you. And you didn't attack Noah, did you?"

"No, of course I didn't."

I got what he was saying. But the thing is, I went out

because I needed to. I had to speak to Lovisa to get her to donate blood. But her coming to the house. That would be great.

"How about we stick to once every five years for me going out?" I said, "as a compromise?"

We laughed, like genuinely laughed, for the first time I can recall in ages.

"How many times did Mum and Dad ring you last night to secretly check up on me?" I asked him. His laugh came to an abrupt stop as he looked at me, quizzically.

"I didn't get any messages. I assumed that she was texting you."

It was my turn to feel confused.

"She didn't contact you at all?"

He shook his head. Both of us were now thinking the same thing: something was up. Lovisa, on the other hand, was far more optimistic.

"This is a good thing, isn't it? Surely it means they trust you. That they knew you'd be okay."

I heard her words, but it was like they were being said in another room. My eyes were locked on Glen's. Mum texts him when he's ten minutes late home from school or when he drives to get pizza, just so she knows how long the wait is going to be. Even though she didn't know there was a party going on, for her to have not contacted either of us all night, well it's just not possible. Not unless there was something wrong.

"We need to ring them right now," I said.

But no sooner had the words left my mouth than Glen's phone began to ring.

Chapter 10

Date: March 4th
Followers: 71

HI GUYS. Thank you for the messages. I know you want an update, and I feel like I need a bit of a distraction, so I'm going to use the time to answer a few more of your questions.

DO YOU HAVE A SOUL?

Okay, pretty deep one to start with there. So, let me ask you this: do you? I'm not trying to be facetious or anything. It's a genuine question. I assumed I had one when I was alive, and given the fact that I love my family and friends just as much as I did then, if not more, I assume I still have one now. Will that do for you?

DO YOU BRUSH YOUR TEETH/FANGS?

Good question, and the answer is yes, but I don't have to. According to Mum's experiments, one of the reasons we stay so perfect is that bacteria and microbes can't exist in or on our bodies, meaning we can't decay or rot. That also means that bacteria can't grow on my teeth and give me foul breath. However, out of habit, I do still clean them (though I'll admit, I do skip a day now and then).

CAN YOU TYPE SUPERFAST?

Another interesting one, and once again, the answer is yes. I can. Now, for the sake of research and because my mum's influence has obviously rubbed off on me far more than I thought, I just did a quick online search which told me that the average speed is 40 words per minute. Then I checked mine, which came out at 200. (Actually 199, but I feel like I should be able to round it up as some of the words were pretty long.) So that puts me at about five times the speed of an average person which is cool, right? That's why I'm able to bash out these blog posts to you so quickly. Particularly the short ones. It might also be a bit of a bonus if I did ever decide I could cope with the idea of carrying on my education and had to write essays again. The only downside is the stress it puts on my computer keyboard and my mobile. I've already ordered a new, industrial-strength screen for this phone as hairline cracks have started to appear in the glass. But really, you win some, you lose some. I can't complain.

DO VAMPIRES HAVE A REFLECTION?

Yes I do. Apparently, the myth of vampires lacking reflections was something to do with the silver backing on old mirrors and us being soulless (see previous answer). I don't know if that's true (the first bit), but I do know I can still see my face every morning when I needlessly brush my teeth!

DO YOU POO?

. . .

Seriously? Is this the level of maturity that we're at on this blog? Although I suppose it's a reasonable question to ask, and the answer is no. I do not.

While the blood travels through my digestive system it is entirely absorbed within the alimentary cannel. (Look at how science-y I sounded there! Mum told me that, though. Sorry if you were starting to think I was super smart. I assure you, I'm not.) So, as I mentioned before, we need all the water as we don't respire, so everything goes straight into my system. All the water from the blood. The iron. The platelets. The hormones. No waste whatsoever. It's pretty efficient, even if I do say so myself. So, put succinctly, no. I don't poo.

CAN YOU SURVIVE UNDERWATER?

Interesting. And I don't actually know the answer. I would think not, but I'm going to be honest, I'm not going to ask Mum to do a test on this one. I think this would go beyond a lot of ethical boundaries. You'll have to find another vampire to answer that one for you. Sorry.

CAN YOU SURVIVE WITHOUT AIR?

• • •

Yes, I can. But … and it's a big but, I can't speak without it. Humans make sounds by passing air over their vocal cords, so if there's no air going in and out, that's not possible. I guess it might explain why so many vampires in films have husky voices though … just a thought.

CAN VAMPIRES GROW LIMBS BACK?

At this point I would just like to say that I am incredible grateful that my mother is the one in charge of the experiments and not one of you guys. Honestly? You think we'd test something like that. I have no idea. But I'll admit, it would be kinda cool if we could, Gecko Girl. I like that idea.

THIS IS CLEARLY BULLSHIT, I LOOKED UP PROFESSOR DAVID COLT AND HE DOESN'T EXIST.

Less of a question and more of a challenge! LOL. Despite not really expecting anyone to read these posts, right from the start I did consider I should be a little circumspect with my identity. You never know, one of you might be Buffy the Vampire Slayer or a descendent of Van Helsing. So, for your information, I have used real first names, just because I'm not sure I could keep fake ones straight in my head, but some places and all surnames are made up. Starting with mine, COLT. (Bonus point to any followers who can figure out why I chose it). Hopefully that will satisfy your doubts, but if not, I don't really care.

DOESN'T YOUR FAMILY DRIVE YOU MAD? WHY DON'T YOU JUST LEAVE?

This question made me laugh, probably more than it should. Of course, some days they drive me nuts. And some days I just get bored. I do wish I could go outside and feel the heat of the sun on my face—without lashings of sunscreen blocking it—but that's just not possible, so I make do. I think the other reason I'm so okay with it, is because of how long I was sick and how tough that was. Honestly, it's hard to know which was more stressful for my family, the cancer or the vampirism. And that might sound ridiculous to someone who's not been through it, but that's the truth. There was so much doubt back then. So many unspoken worries. Now it's not quite like that. Yes, I'm dead, but we know that, and Mum's doing what she can to make it as easy as possible.

Okay, Glen is coming. I'll catch you up later.

Chapter 11

Date: March 5th
Followers: 79

I'M SORRY, I know I said I was going to fill you in yesterday, but honestly, it all got a bit too much. When I got in the car, I gave myself a massive dose of tranquilliser, just so I could block it all out for a while. I know, it's probably not a healthy way of dealing with my issues, but right then I couldn't care less about that. I wasn't the priority. Dad was.

The time at the hospital was intense. Mum didn't want us to come. In fact, she pretty much insisted that we didn't, but she should have had more sense than to think we'd listen to her on something like this. No matter how terrified I was.

We arrived at midday. I was coated head to toe in SPF 100 and was wearing a hoody, jeans, and a face mask, all to try and limit my exposure to the sun. It works well enough if it's not a midday in the middle of summer. That said, I can still feel the effects. It's a kind of tingle, but bearable. The smells, on the other hand, were an entirely different matter.

The moment we stepped through the doors, the scent of blood was so strong, so intense, it was almost overwhelming.

"You don't have to come in," Glen said, taking my hand and squeezing it. "You can wait in the car. I can call you when I'm in there."

I shook my head, swallowing the saliva that was building up in my mouth and feeling the tingle in my fangs as they longed to be released.

When we took the lift, the scents died down by a fraction, but that didn't do anything to help alleviate my nerves.

We walked through A&E (That's Emergency Room for those of you in the US), and I sensed straight away that at least six people in there had open wounds. I didn't need to see them to know. One was barely in his teens. Yup, I can tell all that just from their smell. (And I could pick out a vegan in a taste test any day of the week.)

"You've got this," Glen said. "Lock in on me, okay. I'm the only person here you need to think about."

"This was a bad idea," I said, voicing the thought that had been growing since we first entered the building.

"We won't stay for long. Just check he's okay. See if there's anything Mum needs. I promise, I'll get you out of here as soon as I can."

"Did she not tell you anything? Did she not say what was wrong with him at all?"

"I don't know any more than you do. I'm sure it'll be okay. She would have said on the phone if it was really bad. She'd have told us to come straight in."

I clung desperately to Glen's hand and forced myself to breath in and out loud enough to give me something else to focus on. As he gave the nurse our dad's name, I pressed myself close to him, only moving after I heard the room number and directions.

"This one," I said, as we reached one of the many nondescript rooms along the corridor. No one was speaking inside, but that didn't matter. I'd know my parents' aroma anywhere.

Glen nodded. And we pushed open the door.

I don't know what I was expecting, but it's fair to say that the scene we were faced with was pretty much a nightmare for me. Mum was sitting in a tub chair, reading her book, while my dad was on the bed, propped upright on a load of pillows. A newspaper was open on his lap, but his head was tilted to the side, and his eyes were closed. But most distressing was the canula in his arm, hooked up to a blood bag.

"What happened?" Glen asked, releasing my hand and going up to him.

I remained frozen in the doorway. The smell hadn't yet registered with me. All I could focus on was my father and what the hell was wrong with him.

"Merrewyn? Glen? What on earth are you doing here? I told you not to come."

"You can't tell us Dad's been taken to hospital and then tell us to keep away," Glen said, marching into the room.

His heart thudded as it pumped someone else's blood around his body.

"What's wrong with him?" I said when I finally managed to speak, though it came out as barely a whisper.

While I continued to stare, Glen moved over to Mum, leaned down and wrapped his arms around her.

"We won't stay long," he told her. We just wanted to check you were okay."

"What's wrong with him?" I asked again, my voice becoming slightly more strained.

This time, my mother answered.

"It's not as bad as it looks, honestly. He's just a bit tired, that's all."

"You don't give someone a blood transfusion for being a bit tired, Mother," I snapped.

"No. You're right."

She finally closed her book and stood up.

"But I promise you, it's not all that bad. Your father's been feeling quite tired recently, as you know. And yesterday, well, he fainted, and I had a bit of difficulty waking him up."

"What the hell is that supposed to mean?" I snapped again, and Glen silenced me with a look.

"They've run some tests, and it turns out he's suffering from severe anaemia."

"Anaemia?"

As a vampire with a mother who's a doctor, the possibility of anaemia is something you don't ignore. Mum, Glen and Dad are all on high-dosage iron tablets, given that they all regularly contribute to my stockpile of blood.

"It can be controlled," she tried to reassure me, "now that we know what the problem is. He's going to need regular blood transfusions, to help his body get back on track."

"Regular?"

"It's fine. It's a standard procedure."

A *but* hovered in the air. I didn't want to be the one to ask. I really didn't. Still it came out anyway.

"What are you not telling us, Mum?"

Her lips twisted and her cheeks drew in as her eyes avoided Glen and me. In the end, they settled on Dad, who was stirring.

"Mum," I said, more firmly.

She turned her head slowly away from Dad and looked at me. Tears were glazing her eyes, ready to fall, and I knew exactly what was coming next.

“It means he can’t donate blood for you anymore, Merrewyn.”

Chapter 12

Date: March 5th
Followers: 89

SO, as many of you realise, I am now back exactly where I started 48 hours ago with too few blood donors to sustain me long term. I've gained Lovisa and lost Dad. It's shit. Really shit.

We left the hospital soon after speaking to Mum, although Glen did do a vending-machine run first to grab her a coffee and a chocolate bar. Then, like I said, I tranqued myself for the journey home, just so I didn't have to look at him and feel any more guilt for how much I am screwing with my family's lives. I mean, let's be honest, no one else is going to say it, so I will. I caused my dad to be in this state. Constantly needing him to donate blood is bound to be why this happened, even though Mum and Glen will both insist it wasn't. And what if the same happens to them or Lovisa? Is everyone supposed to put their lives at risk for me?

I can't think about it anymore right now. It's just all too much.

Chapter 13

Date: March 6th
Followers: 98

I'M sorry about how short the last post was. I just couldn't … I couldn't bear to think about it. I was going to tranquilise myself again after I got home from the hospital, but then I remembered that the sedatives are another thing Mum gets hold of through her job. I've no idea how that's going to work now. Not that I use them that often these days. Or at least, I didn't. Something about the current state of play has me thinking I might need them more in the coming weeks.

It's all so freaking shit. And I don't just mean my dad. I mean the entire situation. Like, why would a vampire change me and not stick around for a bit? They could have at least told me where the fuck I could get a decent blood supply from so that I didn't end up draining my parents to the point where one of them has to have freaking blood transfusions. Like WTF? What kind of person does that? I don't care if they're not human anymore. I'm not human anymore and I don't use it as a free pass to be a fucking arsehole.

Okay, breathe Merrewyn. I am not going back down that route again. I got stressed enough yesterday. The whole point of me writing this was so that I could process it and stop being so frustrated and angry.

Like I said, the last couple of days haven't been great. (Understatement of the year.) Basically, take all the emotion you just read about, multiply it by a thousand, and you'll have a fraction of what I was feeling. At one point, I took this little brass paperweight that I've had since I was, like, seven and threw it out the window. I know it wasn't exactly a mature response, and I had no idea how far I can actually throw things. It could have gone off our farm altogether and hit some random dog walker miles away. Not sure how the police would deal with a death like that. As it is, I think I heard it hit one of the barns on the edge of our property, although that could have been my imagination. On the plus side, they're next to the woods, and I don't think they've been used for at least fifty years.

Anyway, Mum has gone to pick Dad up from the

hospital, and as I need a distraction and you have more questions, I thought I would take some time to answer them. It's not like I've got anything else to do.

WHAT TYPE OF BLOOD TASTES BEST?

Ah yes, the taste of blood. Given my comment about DB versus blood bags, I shouldn't really be surprised that you guys wanted an answer to this. Interestingly, what food a person eats can heavily affect how their blood tastes, as do other things, like whether they smoke or drink alcohol. Protein shakes make it taste utterly disgusting, and yes, most old people do have a tang of boiled vegetables, but I don't think that's really their fault. You might be surprised to find out that the most flavourful form of human blood is, in my opinion, from vegans. There's something so utterly pure about it. That probably sounds a bit clichéd, but it's true. It just doesn't taste contaminated.

Another interesting fact is that other chemicals and hormones present also transfer to me. Things like adrenaline and cortisol are often high in first-time donors and can leave me twitchy for days, and while endorphins are generally lacking, when they are there, they taste amazing and chill me out in a way that tranquillisers could never do. High levels of testosterone do all sorts of weird things to me – don't ask.

WHAT DOES LOVISA DO?

So, a bit of a change in direction here, but I get it. It was me talking about her amazing penthouse split-level apartment with views over London, wasn't it? I mean, that place is worth big bucks. Seriously big bucks. Now, as for what she does for a living, it's something to do with investment banking (whatever that is). She's tried to explain it to me, but it doesn't sound all that interesting, if I'm honest. Anyway, through some useful family connections and with a bit of luck thrown in, she and Jamie are sitting pretty.

Now, back to vampire-related questions.

WHY DON'T YOU DRINK ANIMAL BLOOD?

Okay, I'm fairly sure you've got the measure of my mother well enough by now to realise that, obviously, we have tested this. Yes, this topic has been thoroughly researched by trying different types and hoping it wouldn't kill me.

(Okay, that's a little dramatic, but there were days when I wondered exactly how far she would push it, in the name of science.) Anyway, the answer is yes, I can drink animal blood, and it would keep me alive (probably), but it doesn't do me much good and, in fact, I get pretty sick. I think I could go a couple of months on it, but I'm not exactly sure what would happen after that. I guess if we don't find a solution to my blood shortage, then I might find out.

WHAT DO –

Sorry guys. Mum and Dad's car has just pulled into the approach road. I've got to go. I'll post this now and I promise I'll get back to you later and fill you in on everything else.

Take care xoxo Vampire Girl.

(Made me laugh, anyway!)

Chapter 14

Date: March 6th
Followers: 103

HEY I'M BACK. Told you I'd post again, didn't I? Actually, I find it really great having people to talk to about stuff, although I do realise it's a pretty one-sided relationship at the moment. Sorry about that. Maybe when there's less crap going on in my life, I'll have time to learn a bit more about you guys. For now, it's more *Me, Me, Me,* I'm afraid.

Understandably, the moment I was aware that Mum and Dad were close, I yelled to Glen, and I bolted downstairs to meet them. The approach road is pretty long, so we still had a minute for them to reach us, but when the car came into view, I froze. Even when they parked up and Glen raced over to help Dad out, I couldn't move. I just stood there, looking on. The thing is, at first glance, he didn't look like he needed help; he looked pretty much like he always did, although perhaps with a hint less colour in his cheeks than normal. But beneath that, his smell had changed. It had turned sulphury with tangs of chlorine from the two nights stuck in hospital. Maybe I'm being overly dramatic, but the scent of the blood from the transfusions mixed with this made him feel almost like a stranger.

"Dad, I'm so ..." The words caught in my throat as I stepped out onto the gravel and walked towards him. "I'm so sorry if I did this."

"Don't be silly, Ryn."

When he reached me, he pulled my head against his chest, not saying anything, not even moving to brush my hair, just holding me. Heat and cold don't affect me the way they do humans, but as the warmth flooded from him to me, I never wanted to let him go. It was everything my body needed.

"Come on, let's get into the house, Merrewyn," Mum said placing a hand on my arm. "We have things we need to discuss."

You know those TV shows where the families are constantly laughing and happy, and it's all so damn cheery that it's obviously fake? Well, for a while, we had been like that. We had. Even when I was sick, we would still find things to laugh about. We'd curl up together on the sofa under a duvet and watch films on a Friday night. We'd play board games and charades, and no matter what was going on, no matter how much the treatment was taking it out of me or how many hours Mum had been working, there was always a sense of hope in our lives. A feeling that things would turn out right in the end. Sure, that lessened when I died, but it was definitely still there. After all, Mum was doing all these experiments on the rats to try and help me and milking my venom in an attempt to control my urges and testing it, too. It took a couple of years, but eventually our sense of optimism did come back, to some extent at least.

But as we sat around the kitchen table earlier, I truly felt hopeless.

"It's going to be fine," Mum said, as she flicked on the kettle to make them a cup of tea.

I'll be honest, all the stress had made me desperate for a cup of blood, but I didn't drink then, and I still haven't. I need to ration myself more than ever and make what I have last.

"This isn't the end of the world," she said, finally sitting down with us. "You have Lovisa on board as a donor now, don't you? So that means you still have three of us."

"Unless something happens to one of you," I said, bluntly.

"Yes," she agreed.

Surprisingly, the next time she looked up, she didn't look at me but at Glen. Now, I consider myself pretty good at reading between the lines, particularly where my family is concerned, but at that moment, I had no idea what it was they were trying to communicate.

"I think it's time," she said, eventually, before looking to my dad who nodded.

"I agree. I think it is."

Now I want to give you a minute here for you to try to work out WTF they were talking about, because I had no idea. Time for what? For me to go and live with other vampires? Well, that couldn't be it because we'd searched and searched and never found one. Time for me to go and live on my own and feed off rats? No, that was never happening. I honestly had no idea what they were thinking. Loki was weaving his way around my ankles, normally a sure-fire way of getting the strokes that he wants, but this time I couldn't pay him any attention. All the hearts around the table were beating in sync. One thing I already knew was that everyone was in on the secret, except me.

"I'll go get it," Glen said, standing up and disappearing out of the kitchen and up the stairs.

I stared at my parents, willing them to tell me what the hell was going on.

"This is good, Merrewyn," Dad said. "You don't need to look so worried. This is good news."

Good news is definitely subjective.

A minute later, Glen was back and handed me a small paper booklet.

"What's this?" I asked, not even glancing down.

"It's a prospectus. For Aberllaran University."

"Aberllaran?"

"It's on the west coast of Wales," Dad said.

"I know where it is," I snapped back, and my mother's lips twitched, as we both knew that I definitely did not know where it was.

"I've been accepted there to study medicine," Glen continued.

"Glen, that's amazing," I said.

In spite of the shitiness of the situation, I was happy for him. I am happy for him. He deserves it. He deserves every good thing, in fact. And I was just about to stand and go in for a congratulatory hug, when Mum cut in.

"There's something else," she said. "They also offer English Literature. Very small classes. Very small campus. And you've been accepted, too."

If it was actually possible for jaws to hit floors, then mine would have done. Honestly. Like WTF?

"What do you mean, I've been accepted? I didn't even apply."

Glen was grinning now. Mum and Dad were grinning, too. In fact, everyone except me was grinning.

"Attached to the university is a mid-sized clinic that serves the local community," Mum said. "The place runs regular, monthly, blood-donation sessions at the student union there. If Glen volunteers to help out and you put some of that vampire super speed to use, I'm confident you'll be able to … shall we say, liberate enough blood to keep you well stocked?"

"Plus, we'll still bring up blood from Lovisa and your mother when we visit," Dad added.

"So, darling," my mother said, reaching out and taking my hand. "What do you think? The start of your next big adventure?"

"I think you're all insane. For the last seven years we have done our best to limit any kind of contact with people outside this house, and now … what? You want to pack me off to an all-you-can-eat buffet at some remote uni campus in Wales?"

"I know this must be a lot to take in, darling," Mum continued. "This has been in the pipeline for a bit. The trip to see Lovisa was supposed to be the first step to reintegrating you into the world. We were hoping over the next few months we could give you more opportunities to socialise and adjust, so that university wouldn't feel like such a big jump."

"In case you've forgotten, Mum, I'm a vampire. Don't you think people will notice how the new girl doesn't eat or drink and bursts into flames in the sun?"

"Firstly, you don't burst into flames, and secondly, the photosensitivity will cover that. As for eating and drinking, you'll just say you have allergies. All part of the condition."

With Mum clearly convinced this was a great idea, I tried to appeal to my father.

"Dad, surely you can't think it's a good idea? I should stay here. You have to see that?"

"Ryn, Sweetheart," he said, in his most soothing voice, "you are twenty-four, and in a few months your brother will be gone, and you'll be stuck here with just us for company. Eternity is a long time to stay in your room."

I turned my attention to Glen.

"What if I end up feasting on one of your new friends? Or on all of them?"

"You won't. I'll be there to take care of you."

Why was he always so damn reasonable?

"Besides, staying here with no access to enough blood, you'd be a risk to Mum and Dad."

Well played, Glen. Well played.

Chapter 15

Date: March 6th
Followers: 124

WHEN IT BECAME clear that I was not going to win the fight, I came upstairs, hoping that the space would help me formulate a fresh argument. Unfortunately I still haven't come up with anything, but that's not for want of trying. But right now, I've got even more problems to deal with.

If I'd had my head in the game, I would have heard this problem coming. Literally. You know how good my senses are. I can listen in on a conversation on another floor as if I were standing right there with the people or hear a paperweight smashing through a barn roof on the other side of a farm. You can sure as hell bet that I would have been able to hear a car coming up our driveway. But I was so distracted with the blog and everything going through my brain that the first hint I got that someone had arrived at the house was the slamming of the door.

I raced down the stairs and into the dining room where my family was still chatting.

"Everyone, stop talking!" I hissed, praying I was somehow mistaken but knowing I wasn't. Feet were already crunching their way to our front door. Just as they reached it, the scent of the stranger filled my nostrils. Only it wasn't a stranger.

"Noah."

His name escaped my lips as a breathy gasp.

"What?" Mum asked.

"Noah. Fin's brother. He's here. I saw him at Lovisa's. He was at the party."

"You went to a party?"

She looked as if she was about to cry with joy or at least reach out and hug me.

"You didn't say!"

"No. I guess we forgot to mention it. But a lot has been going on since then," I reminded her. "Besides, that doesn't matter right now. What does, is that Noah's going to knock on the door any second. What do we do?"

As if on cue, he knocked.

Glen looked at me with a knowing smirk.

"What's that look for?"

"I'm just wondering how he found out where we live, that's all," he replied, at which point I nearly lunged for him.

"Did you tell him? Did you tell him our address?"

"Don't blame me. I didn't even speak to the guy. He was with you up in the bedroom all night, remember?"

"You spent all night in a bedroom … with a boy?"

At this point, Dad suddenly found enough energy to glower at me, but I didn't have time to put his mind at rest.

"I did not tell him where I lived. Why the hell would I do that? I'm the one who wants to be a recluse, remember? What the hell are we—"

My words were cut short as another, more insistent knock rattled through the house. Mum got to her feet.

"What are you doing?" I said, glaring at her.

"I'm going to let the poor boy in, of course," she replied.

It felt as if I was slipping into some sort of weird vortex. Everything was becoming disconnected.

"You're not answering it," I said, standing in her way. "And there's no way I'm going to."

"You can't just leave him there. He must have travelled miles."

"Then he can travel miles back. Please, if we're all just

really quiet, he might think there's no one in and go away."

"Noah!" Glen's voice came from the hall as he feigned shock. "What a surprise."

"Hey, Glen. Just wondered if Ryn was home?"

"Of course. Come on in."

I was close to hyperventilating (despite not needing oxygen) as my brother led Noah into the dining room, a huge grin plastered across his face. I love him more than anyone, but that doesn't mean I won't beat him to within an inch of his life.

"Noah!"

Mum walked forwards and stretched out her hand.

"What a nice surprise. Ryn didn't tell me she'd bumped into you."

"Did she not?"

It's weird because when I'd seen Noah at Lovisa's I'd been so fixated on Fin—or the fact that he was Fin's brother, that he smelt like Fin, that he reminded me of Fin—that I hadn't really taken the time to notice him properly. On reflection, it's fair to say he had certainly grown up between sixteen and twenty-three. He's one of those guys who suits stubble. You know the type? It just looks really damn good on him. And his eyes were substantially darker than his brother's. Like 70% dark chocolate. Or an espresso. Yup, an espresso fits the colour far better. A playful smile tugged at the corners of his mouth, most irritatingly as it caused about a hundred butterflies to go on the rampage around my insides. I don't know why I wrote that bit. I feel like I shouldn't have. But it's done now, so I'm just going to leave it there and carry on.

At this point, Loki decided he wanted to join in and sidled up to Noah, his old legs hobbling as he walked.

"No way?" Noah said, bending down to give him a stroke. "Is that the same cat?"

"It is," Mum informed him.

"Is he immortal or something?"

"We're starting to think so."

Much to Loki's enjoyment, he continued to pet away. After a minute or so—during which Noah appeared to have completely forgotten the rest of us were there—my mum coughed in the most unsubtle way possible. Noah stood up, blushing, and left Loki to purr around his ankles. It was kinda cute if I'm honest.

"It's very good of you to drop in, Noah," Dad said. "We wouldn't have expected you to come all this way."

"I hope it's okay. I'm actually doing some work not far from here, in Colchester. Lovisa couldn't remember the exact address though, so it took me a while to find you. This place is crazily isolated."

"For a reason," I muttered under my breath, but judging from my mother's glare, she'd heard it clear enough.

"Why don't we go outside?" I said, hoping to get

some privacy away from prying eyes and to ease the horrendous awkwardness of the situation just a bit.

"Outside?" Noah said.

"Yeah, let's go outside."

I whisked him back out through the front door, away from my family's eavesdropping ears.

Considering how early in the year it was, the evening air was surprisingly warm, with feathery clouds that drifted in front of the moon and caused the sky to dim a little each time they passed. Outside our house is not so much a garden as an open field, but in some ways, that's even nicer. My parents put in some flower beds and a pathway and even a bench so that I can go and sit outside at night if I fancy it. Sometimes I do. Not often enough, if I'm honest.

"Your family seemed surprised to see me."

"They're not the only ones," I said, bluntly. "What are you doing here?"

I thought I gave him a pretty intimidating glare when I said this, but he remained as casual as ever.

"Well perhaps if you'd given me your actual phone number then I wouldn't have needed a back-up plan."

At this point I stopped glaring and shifted my weight a little, avoiding his gaze.

"And just a note, you should really practise making up numbers if you're going to do it again. It was so obvious."

"It was not."

"It really was. Why do you think I asked Lovisa for your address before I left?"

"Did you consider for one moment that perhaps I just didn't want to see you again?"

"I can't believe that. I think you should admit it to yourself. You're glad I'm here."

For some reason I can't explain, it was my turn to blush. Vampire style. Which means you probably wouldn't be able to tell by looking at me, but my cheeks burned like hell. I turned around and walked over to my bench, then dropped myself down and began to swing my legs.

"So, you have work near here, do you?" I said, eyeing him suspiciously. "Just happened to be in the area?"

"I do."

"Really?"

"Actually, yes. I will admit, it wasn't meant to begin for a couple of days, but I gave my client a ring and he was happy for me to start on the project a bit earlier."

"How very convenient."

"It was, wasn't it?"

I felt my lips thin as I pressed them together and fought the urge to grin.

Like most nights here, the fields around us were absurdly silent. Sometimes you get the odd noise, an owl hooting, a rabbit scurrying. Now and then, you even get the fox cubs squealing as they play fight, but mainly it's still. And normally all that stillness helps me think. Right then, it really wasn't.

"What are you doing here, Noah?"

"I owe you an apology," he said, looking up at the moon. "A big one." He paused and I wondered if that was it. A moment later, though, he carried on. "When I got home after Lovisa's party, I just kept thinking how hard I'd been on you. That wasn't fair. You didn't ask for any of this."

"No, I didn't."

"You're ill, for crying out loud."

"I know."

'And I was being mad at you for just visiting a friend."

"I know that, too."

"And all that stuff I said about you not coming back, after you'd actually tried. Jeez."

He wasn't looking at the moon any longer, but he wasn't looking at me, either. Instead, his eyes scanned the scene in the near darkness. After a minute he strolled towards me and took a seat at the bench, leaving a gap between us when he sat down. Part of me wished he hadn't. Part of me wished he had sat closer. Just close enough that our knees could touch perhaps. And I suspected he wanted that too, but when his hand moved, it was onto his lap, rather than to take mine.

"Ryn," Noah said. "I know this is all screwed up. Unbelievably screwed up. But it wasn't just Fin who was messed up when you went. I know you never saw me like that, and I get it. I was just a kid—"

"Noah—"

"But I'm not now. And the minute I saw you, I knew none of those old feelings had gone away. They weren't ever going to go away."

I dropped my gaze to the ground with no idea what I was supposed to say to that. Or what I wanted to say. It didn't help that the air was growing more and more stifling by the second. Noah had always been sweet, and that clearly hadn't changed. But other things had, like the broadness of his shoulders, the thickness in his arms, the soft stubble along his jawline and the intensity with which he looked at me. I found myself thinking back to that night all those years ago imagining what the tattoos looked like now, closer up. How they would feel to run my hands over.

I get it. They were not the most decent thoughts to be having, but he was the first guy I'd had a conversation with in a long, long time, so is it really any surprise that I was finding him attractive? But he was also Fin's brother, so maybe that was the reason that it seemed even more messed up. I still missed Fin and thought about him a lot. I think part of me always will.

"Look," he said, breaking into a lighter tone. "I came on a little strong then. How about I take a few steps back?"

"I think you need more than a few steps."

"What about a date?"

"A date?"

"Yes, you know. I take you out. We could go to the cinema or for dinner. Learn a bit more about what we've been up to for these last seven years."

I mulled this over for less than a millisecond before dismissing the idea.

"You live nowhere near here."

"I'm here now, aren't I?"

Honestly, the grin that broke out on his face when he said this caused the butterflies inside me to swarm. Like do a crazy mammoth swarm.

"I'm not sure."

"One date," he whispered. "And if we have a terrible time, I promise you'll never have to see me again."

"Swear?"

"On my life."

His heart was pounding, hammering against his ribs so hard, it felt like it was my own. Despite his cool exterior he was adorably nervous at laying himself open. Swallowing back the heat, I chewed the idea over again. I guess if it went well, we could maybe get some flirty texting going that would help distract me from the endless boredom. If not, then like he said, I'd never have to see him again.

"I'm happy to wait in the car while you make yourself a little more presentable," he added.

Any warm feelings I'd started to have towards him evaporated in that moment.

"Pardon?"

"I said—"

"I heard what you said. How dare you?"

At this point, all his confidence vanished, and he shrank back in on himself.

"Sorry," he said. "I didn't mean to offend you. I just thought you might want to get out of your pyjamas. But if not, I'm fine with that, too. I'm all for comfort wear. Dinner in … those is fine with me."

I looked down and saw he was right. Teddy-bear pyjama bottoms, complete with a week-old red-brown dinner stain. A real winner. I knew then there was no way out of it.

"I'm not much for eating out these days," I said, annoyed by the little smile of victory that adorned his lips.

"Cinema then?" he suggested, then shook his head. "No. No good for chatting. What about bowling?"

"Bowling?"

"You like bowling?"

"It's been a while."

"Then I'll probably kick your arse."

"Unlikely," I scoffed.

My lips were contorted in a weird, almost painful manner, and it took a second for me to realise that I was actually grinning.

"Give me twenty minutes," I said and bolted back through the front door and into the kitchen.

"Mum, Dad I'm going on a date with Noah," I yelled, as I ran upstairs.

So that's it. I'm upstairs in my room, hair wrapped in a towel, typing faster than I ever thought possible.

Ladies and gentlemen, this vampire is about to go bowling!

Chapter 16

Date: March 7th
Followers: 181

WOW! I can't believe how many new followers I've got! That's crazy. As is the number of times you've messaged me asking about my date. Guys, chill. I'll get to it. I will. Although, first of all, I want to address one issue …

I was not being *all dreamy* about Noah's eyes the other day. I was just mentioning them. Pointing out the differences between his and Fin's. That was all. However, now I can confirm that they are amazing and yes, I am totally in over my head, and I have no freaking idea what I'm doing, other than setting myself up for a massive fall.

I'll be honest with you, I never thought I'd be so grateful for having a blog, but it's actually really awesome to have you lot to share this with. I've not really got anyone I can talk to Noah about. I'm tempted to not even tell Lovisa. Not for a bit, at least. See how long she can hold out without mentioning to me that she gave him our address. I should be so mad at her, but it's tough because I really did have a good night.

And yes, of course I'm going to tell you about it. So, sit yourselves down; this might end up being quite a long one …

Twenty minutes and a dozen outfit changes later, I was back in the original combination of blue jeans and white vest top that had been my first choice. Add to that a bit of lippy and a spritz of perfume and I headed downstairs.

Mum was crazily excited. She even gave me an uncharacteristic peck on the cheek before I left.

"Listen to his heartbeat and, you know … smell his sweat, that type of thing. See if he's trustworthy," she whispered. "With a bit of time, you might be able to bring him onboard as a donor. Maybe this is a sign, Merrewyn."

"You want me to smell his sweat so I can decide whether to trust him or not?" I replied as I watched Noah walking to his car.

"You have good senses; use them."

"I'll see you later, Mum," I said, refusing to be drawn any further into her ridiculousness.

My father had fallen asleep in the rocking chair.

"Give Dad a kiss goodnight for me."

"Have fun!" Glen yelled from the top of the stairs. "Don't do anything I wouldn't."

It's fair to say that when I climbed into Noah's car, the excitement was replaced almost immediately by trepidation. It was small and clammy, and when I looked over at him, I could see the pulse of his carotid artery beating faintly in his neck. I couldn't take my eyes off it. And his smell. My God, my fangs are tingling right now just thinking about it.

"You look nice," he grinned.

"Thanks. Sorry I took so long. It's my first date in a while."

"A while?"

"Well, seven years."

He laughed, assuming I was joking, then saw from my face that I wasn't.

"You must have gone on at least one date since then, surely?" he said, but when my expression didn't change, his smile dropped. "It's really been that bad?"

"Yep."

He clutched the steering wheel, speechless, only for his sheepish grin to return in a matter of seconds.

"Great," he said. "No pressure then," and started up the engine.

We slipped into an easy, safe conversation about family.

"I never really understood what your dad does for work," he said. "Fin tried to explain it once. He made him sound like Indiana Jones."

"If Indiana Jones had zero people skills, spent three quarters of his life staring at books and hated adventures, then yeah, that's pretty much spot on. What about your mum? How's she been doing?"

There was a slight pause as his gaze drifted momentarily away before coming back to me.

"It's been tough for her. Losing my gran was hard. Then Fin disappearing off the face of the planet didn't help. She keeps working all the hours God sends, though. First she said it was to pay for Gran's care, then it was to put me through art college. But all that's done now, and she's still at it. I think she's afraid of what'll happen to her if she stops."

"I don't think that's unusual. I can see my mum being the same."

He sighed and nodded.

"I thought it would be better when Fin came back, but the stress that caused …"

His voice trailed off. There's no denying that name was clearly an elephant in the room (well car), and I'd been wondering exactly how long we could go without bringing him up. But given that Noah had now done that, I decided just to go for it.

"So where is he?" I asked, trying to sound as casual as possible. "What's he up to?"

He grinned and I knew he'd seen straight through me, but it had either been that or not mention him all night.

"I wondered how long it would take you to ask about him."

"You brought him up first," I said.

"You're right. I did. He's doing okay, I think. Single now. Divorced. Or at least he was the last time I heard from him."

"Divorced?"

My stomach twisted.

"Yup, you didn't see that coming, did you? Neither did we. He came back from his travels with long hair and this girl. Announced that they'd got married in Vegas just after they met. But it was clear she wasn't a keeper. Seriously crazy. Fortunately I was able to make him see her true colours, not that he thanked me for it. Anyway, three months after they met and she was gone, that was the last we saw of her."

"Sounds messy.'

"Honestly, I don't know. I don't think he knew what he was doing with her. I think he just wanted someone to replace what he'd lost."

"What he'd lost?" I asked.

He looked at me, pointedly.

"Me?"

"You," he said quietly. "From what I gather, there've been a couple of other girlfriends, but it always ends the same way."

"Which is?"

"They want more than he can give."

After that, I could feel an awkward silence building, so I perked up my voice and attempted to be as jovial as possible.

"What's he doing for work now?"

"Teaching, I think. We've kinda drifted apart a bit. He's pretty cagey about his life in general. But I know he qualified as a teacher, so I'm guessing that's what he's doing, but I honestly don't know for sure. "

The narrow country lanes were dark, and it wasn't exactly an incredible view, but I soaked it all in. After all, this was only my third time out of the house in seven years, remember. I was staring up at the moon when Noah spoke again.

"Okay, so I did a Google search while you were getting ready, and it seems there's a bowling alley about six miles away. I hope you remembered your socks."

"Naturally. I'm wearing my lucky ones, in fact."

"Good, because you're going to need all the help you can get."

He was trying to be light-hearted, but I could tell the conversation about Fin had made him tense.

"So, what about you?" I asked. "There was that girl you came to Lovisa's with. How would she feel about you taking me bowling?"

"She's just a friend, that's all. Nothing serious."

For the first time all evening, his pulse quickened and something about his scent shifted. (I've just realised how gross that sentence seems, written down, but hey, this is a no-holds-barred blog.) Anyway, it was obvious he was lying, which put me in a pretty crappy position. For a moment I considered calling him out on it. Telling him that I wasn't interested in getting caught up in some romantic drama, but there again, it wasn't like I actually wanted anything from him. We were just friends going bowling. Technically, he had used the word *date,* but date can be used in different contexts, remember, and I was just thinking of this as more of an adult play date. (God that sounds bad, too. You know what I mean.)

Anyway, after those initially strained couple of minutes, I brought up the subject of the band, and then we got onto what music we were currently listening to, and that was it. We were chatting away like old friends, which I guess we were, talking about everything from the clothes we used to wear to the songs we used to cover and everything in between. In fact, the conversation was so easy, I couldn't believe it when he signalled off the main road and turned into a retail park, where the bowling alley was situated.

"Right, this is us," he said.

Only then did I realised I had a way bigger issue than ex-boyfriends and girlfriends to deal with.

"Shit."

Noah's words echoed my thoughts exactly.

"This isn't good is it?"

"No," I replied. "This is not ideal."

Like I already said, the bowling alley was on a retail park located on the outskirts of town. There are a few big chains stores there and a couple of places to eat, but it's the bowling alley that grabbed our attention. Firstly, that we'd found the place but, secondly, the whole thing was lit up like a Christmas tree. Now I know I've said that I'm okay with every-day light bulbs, and I am. But a lot of these weren't that. I could tell just by looking that there were UV lights outside and likely to be a fair few more inside, too. UV, for those of you who've come to my blog for a science lesson as well as to hear about my vampire catastrophes, is the same high-energy light that the sun emits. The type that causes you to sunburn. Or, in my case, seriously burn.

"How much light can you handle?" he asked.

"Not this much."

"Do you think you'll be all right inside?"

"I doubt it."

His face fell.

"I mean, I might be okay for ten minutes or so," I

said, trying to sound positive. "I did put a bit of sunscreen on, but not loads as it's night-time. We could still probably have a really quick game."

With his hands on the door, he scoffed. "I did not wait nine years for our first date for it to be *really quick,*" he said. "Wait right here. I'll be back in a minute."

"Why? What are you going to do?"

"You'll see."

And with that, he got out of the car and left me on my own.

It was the first time, I realised, that I had ever been left alone in a populated area. Not that it was busy, but there were enough people around to put me on edge. A group of teens was milling about, and an older couple was strolling along, arm in arm. A homeless man then held my attention as he wheeled a trolly full of plastic bags past the restaurant. He was leaning so heavily on the handle as he shuffled along that I wondered if he'd be able to even stand without it. Every step seemed impossibly slow and painful. But it was his clothes that really caught my attention. He was wearing a full-length cloak with a hood. I wondered where he'd stumbled across something like that. Maybe it had been given to him or perhaps it was something he clung onto from his former life. Either way, I continued to dwell on it until he wheeled himself around the corner and out of sight.

That was when I looked back towards the bowling alley and noticed that something was different. It was not until I saw Noah walking towards me with half-a-dozen people strolling out behind him, that I realised what it was. The building was in total darkness.

"Come on," he said, opening the door for me to get out. "We're good to go."

Chapter 17

Date: March 7th
Followers: 195

I KNOW, I know. I didn't finish the story, but there's quite a lot to get through, and I have other things to do. Like read. And play the drums. And lie on the sofa like the teenager that I physically am … and go over and over every last detail of the date because my memory is freaking awesome.

Anyway, I'm back to tell you more now. Loki is actually on the bed with me, purring like a kitten as I write this, which is really cute. Seriously, I love this cat.

Right, back to my date.

As I previously said, Noah stepped out of a blacked-out bowling alley and walked back to the car to fetch me.

"What did you do?" I asked when he opened the door.

He shrugged in that casually evasive way he has, which I am already finding chest-burningly cute.

"It was nothing. It's a Monday night. There were five people playing in there. So I offered to buy them all pizza if they'd leave, then shouted the manager another one for switching the lights off. They've got to leave a few on, I'm afraid. Health and safety stuff, but it should buy you a fair bit longer."

"You got them to switch off all the lights at a bowling alley so that I could have a game?"

"Almost all."

The burning in my chest transformed into an overwhelming ache that clamped itself around my lungs in a way I didn't think was possible.

"Thank you," I finally managed to say.

Inside the alley, and I'm not joking here, it looked like one of those scenes from a rom-com. You know, where the whole place is lit up with fairy lights and little round candles in jam jars and there's all this slow music going on in the background. Many of the lights were shaped like bowling pins, and the "fairy" lights were red and there to mark out the lanes, and the music was some cheesy dance remix, but hey, it was the closest I've ever got to a romantic evening, that's for sure.

We headed over to change our shoes into the blue-and-red clown ones they always give you.

"What size do you need?" the boy behind the counter asked.

He was probably the same age as Glen with freckled cheeks and ears a fraction too big for his head.

"Ryn, meet Craig, the duty manager this evening and the kind sir who graciously switched off all the lights for us."

"I can't believe you did that."

"It's no problem. We were pretty dead anyway. Besides, it's bound to win me some brownie points with the girlfriend when I tell her. What size was it you needed?"

"Seven," I said.

Noah smirked as Craig turned to grab me the shoes.

"What?" I said. "What's so funny?"

"Nothing. I like a lady with big feet," he laughed.

So to show him exactly what my big feet were capable of, I playfully tried to kick him.

"You do get feisty," he said, jumping out the way.

"You don't know the half of it."

As we sat on a bench doing up our laces, I felt compelled to ask him about what he'd told me earlier.

"In the car," I said, trying to sound casual, "you told me you'd been waiting for this date for nine years."

"I did."

"Did you mean it?"

I continued to battle with the laces. Why this place didn't use Velcro straps, I have no idea. When I was finally done and looked up, he was staring straight at me.

"Of course I meant it."

"Honestly?"

I couldn't hide my surprise.

"First band practice. You remember? When Lovisa was singing and we couldn't keep in time with one another, but you just wouldn't give up?"

"I remember."

"You were the only one of us who knew what the hell they were doing, and you were beating the drums like your life depended on it, desperately trying to get us in time."

"I was actually so pissed off."

"I know. Seriously, it was hot."

"You were like, ten?"

"I was thirteen, nearly fourteen and just as charming then as I am now, I'm sure."

It was impossible not to laugh as I recalled the sandy-haired boy with a bass guitar that looked three times too big for him.

"I don't quite remember that."

"Of course you don't. You didn't notice me at all once Fin came onto the scene."

I pressed my lips together and said nothing. There was no point denying it.

"For a few weeks, I actually thought I still stood a

chance," he carried on. "Particularly as he was doing the whole deep-and-moody act. I thought it would give me some time to win you over with my humour. But I knew, sooner or later, you'd talk to him, and he'd fall hook, line and sinker."

"Wow."

I literally had no idea what else I could say to this massive declaration. I mean, it was insane. And he didn't stop there.

"You were the crush of my life. And it didn't stop when you two got together. Even when you started dating, I was sure he was going to screw it up at some point or you'd grow bored of all his broodiness, so I planned on being right there, ready to sweep you off your feet. Although my plan didn't quite work."

"Because I never got bored of him?"

"You didn't, did you?"

An awkwardness was starting to bloom, but before it could settle he grabbed me by the hand and pulled me over to the alley.

"Right, pick your name. I'm going for Noah the Dream Date," he said, typing it onto the scoreboard.

"Seriously?"

"I think I've earned it."

He began typing again.

"And for you, Ryn the Vampire?"

"What?"

Every muscle in my body went rigid. My fangs began to tingle.

"Why would you say that?"

"You know, cos you can't go out in the light or anything. Surely I can't have been the first person to make that joke."

"First and last."

He thought I was joking, until he noted my locked jaw and clenched fists and hastily pressed delete.

"Okay. Clearly some bad judgement on my part there. How about just Noah and Ryn? Does that work better for you?"

"Much better," I said.

Now what followed, ladies and gents, was my first and only major faux pas of the night. I don't really have an excuse. I just wasn't thinking. With the screen ready and the pins waiting at the end of the lane, I reached down, grabbed the nearest ball and shook it in his face.

"Are you ready to get your arse whooped?" I said.

Noah squinted and stepped towards me.

"Shit, Ryn, have you been secretly working out for the last seven years or something?"

"Why?" I said, confused at where the comment had come from. (I do actually have a weight bench, but it's mainly used by Glen or to throw clothes on when I can't be bothered to put them away.)

"That's a sixteen-pounder you're waving around there," he said, staring at it.

"It is?"

I lowered my hand and saw that, sure enough, the number 16 was in bold print right on the top.

"I guess they must have labelled it wrong," I said, then before he could check sent it hurtling down the lane for a perfect strike. "Works all right though," I added, with a grin.

I'm not going to lie to you, bowling with vampire senses is pretty straight forward. Gone are the days when I used to struggle to hit even one pin. Now, it's harder *not* to knock them over. All the while we played, we were chatting away like we'd been best buddies forever.

"Most underrated superhero?" he asked.

"Daredevil. Understated and witty. And kick arse."

"Most overrated?"

"Definitely Iron Man."

"You have to be kidding. He died saving the planet."

"And was a dick most of the time."

"Okay, favourite action film?"

"I'm not into them."

"What?"

His jaw dropped in mock horror.

"How can you not love a good action film."

"Because they're all the same. The man overcomes his emotional inadequacies to get the girl and save the day. Nope, I'd rather read a book."

"Right, it is now my mission to give you a complete film education."

"I don't think I'm the one who needs educating, thank you. Trust me, I've watched enough of them to know they're all the same."

"But that's what makes them great. The way the tropes are developed and exposed. Come on, you've got to at least let me try to show you why they're the best genre."

I half-heartedly agreed, mainly because I was worried we'd never get to the end of the game if we didn't get on with it.

Now, if you think I was all demure and did the whole let-the-man-win thing, then you haven't learned much about me yet. I'll admit I did let him believe he'd got a sliver of a chance a couple of times, but win? No way. When the last balls had been thrown and the remaining pins scooped up, I finished a full 57 points ahead of him.

"Beginner's luck," he said. "It's got to be."

"Maybe you should just stick to painting."

He flinched.

"That's it. Round two and I'm not taking no for an answer."

"You really think you'll beat me?"

"Like I said, beginner's luck. I've warmed up now."

"If you're sure … although I warn you, it's way more embarrassing to have your arse kicked twice."

"I'll take that chance."

He'd just brushed past me to reset the game when Craig appeared.

"Sorry," he said. "Gotta shut up now."

"Really?" Noah gave him the most pleading look possible. "We can't squeeze in one more game?"

With what I suspect was his most managerial expression, he shook his head.

"These things are time logged. I'll already be on dodgy ground with the manager if she finds out I switched all the lights off. She'll have my balls in a bag if I don't shut up on time, too. Besides, I need to take my girlfriend out for that pizza you so kindly offered to pay for."

With a glance in my direction, Noah sighed.

"I guess I'll just have to think of another way to entertain you," he said.

It would be wrong not to admit that I might have felt a slight fluttering of excitement when he said that. Although the truth was, I knew I could do with heading back. It's not that I needed blood—I'd brought my trusty hip flask with me just in case—it was that the more time we spent together, the more I didn't want the evening to end and the more that worried me. You see, he made me laugh far more than Fin ever did, and therein lay the problem. I kept comparing them. And it didn't seem right to carry on like that.

As we handed our clown shoes back to Craig—who had now been joined by his girlfriend—and took our own, I decided this was an appropriate time to call an end to the night.

"Would you be okay driving me home now?" I said. "I think my body's taken as much as it can handle for one evening."

"Already?"

I'll be honest, the disappointment in his face made me want to back track, because we were having an incredible time, but I managed to hold my resolve.

"Okay," he said and handed me his car keys. "Why don't you go get in the car? I need to use the toilet."

"I'll wait."

"Honestly, it's fine. I need to settle up with Craig as well. I won't be long."

So, taking the keys from him, I left the most romantic date setting I'm ever likely to experience and waited for him outside. Even for someone who lives in the middle of nowhere, I found the carpark eerily quiet. The lights were on in the nearby pizza place and a low bassline reverberated from somewhere, but the carpark itself was empty. Even the homeless guy had gone off with his trolley. Fortunately, I only had to wait a couple of minutes before Noah joined me.

"You sure I can't tempt you to stay out any later?" he asked, taking the keys and slipping them in the ignition.

"Not tonight," I replied without thinking.

"Not tonight?"

He raised his eyebrows.

"Can I infer from that you might be willing to accept the offer of another date?"

Even now I don't know if I made the right call. Actually, I'm pretty sure I didn't. But I gave the answer I wanted to at that precise moment.

"I think that could be fun," I said.

On the drive back, we carried on chatting away, although I was finding it a bit trickier to focus. It was the end of our first date, after all, and we were both, technically speaking, in our twenties and I was kind of worried/petrified that he might be expecting us to kiss or something. There'd been none of it at the bowling alley. Not even a hint. But there'd been lots of flirting, hand touching, fingers meeting, high fives and even a surprise hug after one strike. Now don't get me wrong, as a human I liked kissing. A lot. But I'm not anymore. And I couldn't shake off the thought that my fangs might pop out mid-snog. Which is why, when I reached the turn-off for our house, I told him I'd get out and walk the rest of the way.

"You can't be serious?" he said, "It's miles." (He wasn't wrong.)

"Honestly, it's not that far. And I like to walk." (Complete lie.)

"Well, let me walk with you."

I shook my head.

"Then you'd have to walk all the way back. Honestly, it's fine. I'm fine."

For the first time since the drive there, the pair of us fell into an uneasy silence. Well, silent for him at least. All

I could focus on was the rhythm of his heartbeat, that was getting faster and faster, and the way his shoulders, whether subconsciously or not, were starting to tilt forwards. I could see his head and lips moving closer to mine any second.

Now I may be lacking real-life experience in the dating arena over the last few years, but I have seen every romcom that Netflix has to offer and I know exactly what it means when two young people are sitting silently in a car after going on what was, undeniably, a bloody awesome date. I knew that any moment he was going to be lean forward. Press his lips against mine. And although biting him was the farthest thing from my mind the fact was, the excitement was driving all sorts of feelings in me and my fangs were itching to break free. I didn't know what to do. So I quickly pecked him on the cheek and jumped out the door, no doubt leaving him wondering what the hell had just happened.

So there you go. That's all there is to tell. For now at least.

Chapter 18

Date: March 8th
Followers: 2780

WTF YOU GUYS, where the hell have all these new follows come from? And why have I got five hundred messages on here?????

Look, I don't know what's brought this on. I've been in bed most of the day and only just gotten up. I'll post properly when I know what's going on. (Although, if I've reached influencer status, does that mean I can ask for free shit?) Ignore I just said that. Your messages are still pinging through. I need to find out what on earth is happening.

Chapter 19

Date: March 8th
Followers: 3207

OKAY, now I understand. I didn't read them all, but trust me, I read enough. More than enough. Now I need a drink. And I don't mean blood. I need hard liquor of the thirty-percent-proof-or-more kind. I don't have a clue what it would do to me as I haven't been drunk since my seventeenth birthday, but I don't really care. My head's already spinning. I can't imagine that having a drink or two is going to make any difference. There's just too much to take in right now.

Chapter 20

Date: March 9th
Followers: 3215

SORRY I'VE BEEN absent since yesterday. I've had a lot to get my head around. One hell of a lot.

I don't know where to start, but I'll have to try. So here goes.

For those of you who are on here now but have missed all the major drama (I don't know how you've managed that given the number of comments, but hey, I'll fill you in anyway), the police have released a report saying that there were three murders at a bowling alley in Essex on Monday night. I've checked the papers and watched the news. It's the same place. It's the one that Noah and I were at. I just can't process it.

Seriously, fuck. It's horrible. In fact, it's worse than that. I can't explain how I feel right now. I don't even want to be writing this blog. But there's something on here I had to respond to. Something I needed to say. Because things are already out of control.

I've received over six hundred hate messages in the last three hours. I'm not kidding. Over six hundred. Forty-eight hours ago I didn't have even half that many followers. But now you're here, and you all seem to think I'm the one to blame for these deaths. Well I'm not.

I didn't have to tell you about my life. I didn't have to tell you the truth about what I am and what I've been through. I didn't have to tell you about Noah and our date and where we went. Not once have I lied on this blog. And I'm not now. The only thing the papers say is that there was massive blood loss. That's it. No bite marks. No drainage. A knife could cause that. Or a gun. Plenty of other things could have led to a death like that. I did not kill those people. And I'm going to prove to you that it wasn't a vampire.

This was not me.

Chapter 21

Date: March 10th
Followers: 4752

WHO KNEW that people thinking you were responsible for killing three people would be the quickest way to grow your blog? Maybe I should share this fact with all those content creators out there? (That's a joke by the way. Honestly, I'm so worried about the conclusions you guys are capable of jumping to, I feel I should double check everything I write. But that's not my style, so I guess I'll have to get over it.)

Firstly, to those of you who've been following me on here from the start, sorry I've been absent for the last twenty-four hours. I'm still trying to process everything.

I'll be honest, I had hoped that when I came back to write this post, it would be to unequivocally prove my innocence to you. But I can't do that. All I can do—all I've ever done—is be truthful. So I'm going to tell you exactly what I know about everything, and you can make your own conclusions from there. I'm not going to keep defending myself to people who don't even want to believe that I'm innocent. You're not worth my time. I do want to give a shout out, though, for those of you who are standing by me. Those of you who have been with me since the beginning and are calling out the trolls. I see you, and I'm grateful. I just hope that you continue to believe me after I tell you what I found out last night.

After finishing up on here, I went to see Glen. Unsurprisingly, he had his head buried in a book while scribbling on a notepad at the same time.

"Hey," I said, taking a seat on the end of his bed. "Have you seen the news today?"

He scoffed and looked up.

"You serious? I missed school on Monday, remember? It's crazy the amount of catch-up work you're left with after just one day absent. Not to mention the fact that my bloody car overheated two miles from school this morning, so I had to come off the road, and now have the first part of my chem lesson to catch up on, too. I've seen nothing other than the inside of textbooks. I can't wait 'til I am done with these damn exams."

Glen is not someone who rants. He's really not. So

this little outburst was majorly out of character. Seeing the stress he was under, I considered leaving him to it, but then in the grand scheme of things, exams grades vs being accused of murder? Once again, I was definitely the priority.

"I need your help with something," I said, feeling my hands shake as I spoke.

He opened his mouth and looked up again, obviously ready to give me a standard dismissal, but I guess something in my face stopped him.

"Ryn," he said, pushing his books to the side. "What is it? What's happened?

"Remember when we were searching for other vampires?" I said.

"It's hard to forget. I thought I was going to end up on the FBI's most wanted hacker list with some of the things you made me do."

"I know. But the thing is, I need you to log on to the Essex Police data base," I said. "I need you to find out about a murder for me."

I saw the hesitation in his eyes and I utterly understood. It was all very well hacking into things when he was a kid, when the worst he might get was a slap on a wrist. But he's got his whole future ahead of him now, and something like that on his record could completely ruin it. For a second I thought he was going to refuse, but he nodded and reached for his laptop.

It didn't take him long. Longer than it would have

done when he was doing it almost daily, but that's hardly surprising. I watched as he typed in a couple of rewrites to avoid firewalls (whatever the hell that means), and he was in there.

"What was the date?" he asked.

"Day before yesterday. It was reported on the eighth."

He typed again.

"Three people were killed," I added.

A minute more and I was starting to get nervous.

"Are you sure nobody will be able to track you?" I asked, as line after line of what looked like complete gibberish appeared on the screen.

"No one is going to know we're here unless they're able to manually decrypt an algorithm that uses polynomial factorials to rewrite itself every millisecond."

"Is that a no?" I asked, needing a bit of human speak.

"We're fine. Now, hold on a second. I think I'm in."

Two seconds later, and he hit the return key with even more force than normal.

"Triple homicide at a retail park?"

"That's it. Can you get up the file?"

No sooner had I asked, than his computer screen filled with official-looking documents, and I was leaning over his shoulder.

"What is it you're looking for?" he asked.

"I don't know. I'll tell you when I see it."

The first details were of a woman, nineteen, the

second a man of the same age, but it was the name that caught my attention. Craig Denvour.

"Craig," I whispered.

"You know him?" he asked, looking back at me.

I'm not sure if I nodded or shook my head or did neither. It was impossible to think about anything other than the nausea that was rising in my throat.

"Are there any photos?" I asked. "There should be shouldn't there?"

"Just give me a minute."

A few clicks later and a series of thumbnails filled the screen.

"No," I gasped.

I didn't need them any bigger. The first was of the interior of the bowling alley, the lights still on low the way they had been when Noah and I left. The second one showed Craig on the floor, his T-shirt splattered with blood. Next to him was a girl. Her skin was grey and translucent, her eyes open wide in fear. Behind them on the table was a half-eaten pizza. They'd not even finished their meal.

"What about the third person?" I asked.

Glen scrolled down to the image of a man slumped over a shopping trolley. The homeless guy.

Without being asked, he clicked on the photo so it expanded to fill whole screen.

"What the hell did that?" he said. "It looks like an animal attack."

It did. Dozens of teeth marks punctured his arms, his shoulders and a cheek, although nowhere were there as many as on his neck. Chunks of flesh were missing, too, showing the bone and muscle underneath.

"That can't have been a vampire," I said, as much to myself as Glen. "It must have been an animal. No vampire would do that."

"Not unless they had no idea what they were doing."

"Zoom in on the other photos," I said, against my better judgement.

Craig's injuries were similar enough for it to be considered the same MO. A massive chunk of his neck was missing, although the rest of his body was relatively unscathed. But the girlfriend was different. Other than teeth marks, the flesh was intact.

We looked at the screen in silence. Every hair on my arms was standing on end. I knew Glen was thinking the exact same thing as me. A moment later, he said it.

"It looks like a vampire attack. By one who's just … who's just …'

"Who's just learning how to feed off humans," I finished for him.

Chapter 22

Date: March 11th
Followers: 5558

WOW, you guys aren't giving up on these comments are you? Well just so you know, anyone who posts abuse here from now on is getting blocked immediately. This is a safe space, and that means for others and me too. We don't need people sharing scary BS when there's enough crap out there in the world for us already.

That said, there's no way around the fact that a vampire was responsible for those killings at the bowling alley. It wasn't just the bite marks. Whoever did the post-mortem commented that they looked as if they'd been made by an animal, which is understandable, but they also recorded an unknown toxin in the blood. *Unknown toxin,* as in vampire venom.

This could all be a coincidence, of course. That's what Glen thinks, and he could be right. But we've always been aware that there have to be more vampires out there. Even if it's just the one who turned me. Maybe they went on a killing spree. Or maybe they got lonely and decided to make some new friends—literally—and were teaching them the ropes. It's not a nice thought, I know, but it just doesn't make any sense otherwise. Maybe there are vampire murders every day, and this was just a case of one of them seriously losing control.

Anyway, I'm going to log off here for a few days. All these messages and comments are a lot to deal with right now. Thank you to those of you who are still on my side, though. It really means a lot. I promise I'll let you know if there are any more developments.

Chapter 23

Date: March 13th
Followers: 8911

OKAY, taking a couple of days off was definitely a good idea. And I wish I could carry on this post with some positivity, but there've been some developments today. Seriously concerning developments.

First, I need to say sorry if you sent me a supportive message and I haven't replied. If I'm honest, chatting to you guys has been my favourite part of doing this blog. It almost makes me feel human again, but I just can't handle some of the abuse coming through right now. There are only so many times you can type *Fuck Off* without it getting to you. I'm a vampire, guys, but I still have a heart, even if it doesn't beat or require oxygen. Basically what I'm saying is, even with all my obvious deficiencies, I'm a darn sight nicer than some of you arseholes out there.

While I was changing my settings, I also put mute on all other notifications, so I can't see any of the sick memes and crap that's been filling my inbox. So sorry if you sent something that wasn't sick, but I wiped it all in one go. It was the easiest way.

In the end, this afternoon, I told my dad about what had happened. Not the part about Glen hacking into a police database so that I could view the medical records, but how I stumbled across the news of some deaths that looked remarkably like vampires were involved. Surprisingly, neither Mum nor Dad had picked up on the events despite the fairly heavy media coverage of the murders. Mum's been lost in her own little world the last couple of days. I guess it's to be expected, given what she's been though with Dad and losing her job and everything. Still, it's odd to hear her heart charged up on excess adrenaline. It's so unlike her. So I decided to speak to Dad alone. After all, this is basically his profession. I added a few red herrings though when I spoke to him, just to be safe. For starters, I told him that I'd seen an article on the internet and that it had happened over a year ago and in Scotland, too. But I kept the rest the same. Three deaths, each person maimed to a greater or lesser extent.

"It's highly unlikely," he said, as I followed him into

his study after dinner. "Three people in one night. In the same public location. No. Not a vampire."

"And it couldn't be a pack of them?"

He chuckled briefly, like I was a little kid who'd just said something stupid.

"Vampires have survived millennia living in the shadows. Their continued existence has only been viable because people don't believe they exist. I'll be honest, even I, as a firm believer in the occult, took a while to come to terms with the fact that you genuinely are, you know … dead. If the truth got out, they would be hunted to extinction. Vampires do not draw attention to themselves. To do so would be to sign their own death warrants."

I had to agree with him on that. After all, how many years had I been trying to track one down, with no luck. And it's not like I go out and publicise my existence. (Okay, that's actually exactly what this blog is doing, but just ignore that for the moment. It's not like it's getting me an invite to be on *I'm a Celebrity*. Besides, from all the hate mail, half of you don't believe me anyway.)

"Chances are," he said, "anything you think could be a vampire killing is almost exactly the reason it won't be. They are discreet, they are intelligent, they are—"

"Out there."

"Yes, but so are lots of other things. Human things. War and famine. Radicalised and unstable people. I'm far more worried about being struck by a car than I am of your kind."

He put his hand on my shoulder.

"If you look for the bad in everything it's all you'll ever see, Merrewyn. We both know some highly unusual things are going bump in the night out there, but when you hear hooves, don't let your mind convince you it's zebras."

I was about to reply it wasn't my mind playing tricks, it was the police reports and very clear photo images that would definitely stop him ever eating lasagne again, when a car door slammed.

"For fuck's sake. Again?"

I'll be honest, if I was you right now, I would seriously be starting to doubt whether I actually have that super hearing that I've bragged about, but I swear I can normally hear a car the second it turns onto our drive. The fact was, once again, I'd been way too distracted, and by the time I realised he was here, I also realised there was nothing I could do. A quick listen in on his pulse rate showed it was elevated. He was nervous. Which was good, because so was I.

A moment later the doorbell rang.

"I suppose I should go and get that," I said.

I walked out of Dad's study to find my mother loitering in the hall, and for a second I was reminded of all those years ago when I first started dating Fin. Not that

I'm comparing what Noah and I have with that, obviously.

"Is this a thing?" she asked, standing in front of me with a steely look in her eye. "This is not a great time to be starting something."

"I'm not sure what it is," I replied, as excitement and nausea started battling it out inside me. "Besides you were the one encouraging me to go out. You were excited even."

I watched her nostrils flare as she took a deep breath in.

"Just be careful," she said, then stepped out of view, although I could tell from her heartbeat she was still within listening distance.

I opened the door, expecting Noah's normal coy smile or for him to come out with some witty remark. However, what I actually got was a god-awful smell.

"What the hell is that?" I said, gagging.

Dangling from his hand was a plastic bag, emitting the most heinous smell I have ever encountered. Vampire senses are OTT remember. Think putrid flesh, overflowing toilets. Think someone who has just had the spiciest curry of their life and then … well you get the idea. It was bad. Seriously bad.

"Fish bones," he announced. "For Loki."

"Mum!" I yelled.

I was genuinely concerned that the smell might actually be bad enough to cause my fangs to pop out of their own accord. (It's never happened, but then I'd never smelt anything quite that foul before.) Mum was there by my side in an instant.

"Fish bones," Noah said again. "I'm doing a mural at a fish and chip shop. They were throwing them out."

"Noah. You're back again," my mother said, her eyes beginning to water. "You know cats can't actually eat fish bones, don't you?"

"Can't they?

"Nope."

(I think it's the first time I've ever heard her use the word, but I swear, that's what she said.)

"They can get stuck in their throats and choke them."

"Seriously?"

"Seriously."

Looking more than a little deflated, he looked at the bag in his hand.

"I've had this in my car all the way from Colchester," he said, at which point Mum looked at him like he might possibly be the most stupid person in the world.

"There's a bin out back," I said. "But you're carrying it there."

I pinched my nose and led him around the outside of the house.

"Okay," he said, dropping the bag in the plastic dustbin, where it landed with a thud. "That present was a dud."

"Yeah, we're tricky to buy for in this house. Even the cat."

He attempted a half smile, but I could tell from his puppy-dog eyes that he was as gutted as the fish those bones had come from. He'd obviously thought that winning over Loki would lead to doing the same with me. Which is not a bad game plan, I suppose.

"I thought maybe I could take you out for dinner," he said. "I would have texted, but then I realised I still don't have your real number. I was going to ask Lovisa for it, but I thought you might just ghost me, although I figured that would probably have more to do with the previously-dating-my-brother thing, as opposed to not wanting to see me again. At least that was the impression I got just before you bolted out of the car the other night."

"I did not bolt."

"That was a definite bolt."

"A slow sprint, at most."

"Can you have that? Surely, you're either sprinting or you're not?"

His slanting smirk was back, which I found amazingly reassuring.

"I've actually just eaten," I replied, in answer to his earlier comment. "And my condition means I have a pretty restricted diet anyway."

(See what I did there? No word of a lie.) I did feel rather bad about turning down his offer, but I had a solution. One that didn't even require leaving home.

"What are you like at board games?" I asked.

The thing is, I really do love them. And cards. Which is why that incident with Glen and the compound fracture and the subsequent banning of any form of competition in the house was a real downer for me. But there was no rule in place that said I couldn't play games on a date in the garden.

Given the clear skies, and my utter imperviousness to cold, we sat on the patio at a table I'd barely used previously. After a couple of rounds of Scrabble, we tried some other lesser known games I'd collected and had to explain the rules to. Catan, Tiny Towns. That type of thing. Eventually we moved on to poker.

"Why are you doing that?" he asked, as I raised the stakes and pushed another matchstick into the pile. "You said you'd played this game before."

"It's called tactics," I replied. "I've got a plan."

"If it's for me to wipe you out and take all your money with the next hand, you're doing pretty well."

"We'll see."

"Yeah, we will."

I lost the next hand and the one that followed.

"How much is that you owe me?" he laughed and threw his cards down.

He reached over to collect up the rest of the pack, then stopped.

"Is it me or do the curtains keep moving?"

I glanced over and they were indeed twitching.

Throughout the course of the evening, I'd seen all their faces: Mum, Dad and Glen, peering out. Which is really stupid because any of them could have joined us. The more the merrier when it comes to playing games.

"So, how long is this going to go on for?" I asked, as he shuffled for another game.

"What, cards? I'm happy to keep whooping your arse. Consider it payback for the bowling."

"I mean you turning up like this. Uninvited. Surely you have other places you need to go?"

"There's nowhere else I'd rather be," he replied.

"What about your girlfriend?"

He shrugged, wrinkling his nose a little.

"There's no one special. Not really."

I offered him my most withering look.

"Listen, I don't know what your plan is, turning up like this, but I'm guessing Fin has no idea you're here. And I'm okay with that. For now. But if there's someone else in the picture then I'm not interested. My life is already way too complicated at the minute."

That obviously hit home, and he lowered his gaze momentarily before lifting it up to meet mine.

"Okay. I get it. I should be honest. I was seeing some-one. Was. Past tense. But it's over now. Done and dusted. Or least it is at my end. One hundred percent. Breakups can be tricky sometimes, you know?"

I don't. The only one I've experienced is the type where you're medically sedated for so long your boyfriend forgets you exist. Still, I nodded like I had a clue. I was fairly certain that an awkward silence was about to follow, but just then his phone rang, saving us both.

He glanced down at the screen, as did I (all that appeared there was the letter A, which didn't tell me much).

"Sorry, I need to answer this," he said and stood up. "You don't mind, do you?"

"No, of course not," I replied, knowing full well I was going to listen in. "I'll shuffle these properly while you're gone."

I picked up the deck, split it in half and did a perfect riffle shuffle.

"You just keeping getting cooler don't you?"

"Quite possibly," I said. "Now answer the phone."

He held my gaze for a fraction longer than normal.

"You have no idea how infuriating you are," he said, before sauntering off around the side of the house.

I was just about to tune in when a banging on the back window eclipsed his voice. I looked over to see Glen there with his mouth pressed against the glass, making what I can only describe as a gross impersonation of someone kissing. I gave him a tight smile and the middle finger, only for my mum to pull the curtain aside at that exact moment. She was still glaring at me when Noah came back around the corner looking decidedly paler than before.

"Everything okay?" I asked.

"Yeah, it's fine. It will be fine. Nothing to worry about."

Then he looked up to the sky and gave a long shudder.

"Is it okay if we move inside?" he asked. "I'm getting pretty cold. Aren't you?"

I shook my head.

"I tend not feel it that much. A side effect of the medication," I added.

"Well, speaking as someone who's warm blooded, can we relocate somewhere a fraction less chilly? We can sit in the car if you don't want to go indoors."

The idea of sitting in a car with a boy on my parents' drive definitely brought back memories. Like one time when Fin and I had gone to see a movie together, only to miss the film because we got so wrapped up in kissing and what can best be described as heavy petting. Needless to say, they weren't memories I fancied sharing with Noah, either, particularly as my mum had just come out of the house with a rubbish bag—a clear ploy to try and get a better view of what we were up to.

"Just one more game," I said, "then you can go."

"Wow, great hostess skills there, Ryn."

"Says the visitor who keeps turning up uninvited."

I had just finished dealing when a scream shot through the night air. Never in all my life have a heard one like it. It was as if someone's lungs were exploding from their chest.

Simultaneously we jumped to our feet.

"Mum!"

I bolted across the lawn in a millisecond, following the direction the sound had come from, not even considering hiding my vampire speed. I didn't think about anything other than getting to Mum. When I turned the corner of the house and saw her panting on the ground, I gasped with relief.

"What is it? What happened?"

She was kneeling by the bins, and for a second I thought she'd slipped and hurt herself, but then I saw what was in front of her.

"Is that Loki?"

She couldn't say anything. Her breathes were juddering gasps. Our cat was spread out on the ground, and if it wasn't for Mum being in such a state, I would have thought he was just sleeping. Everything about him was relaxed, even his lips appear to be curled upwards in a smile.

"What's wrong?" Noah asked, arriving at my side. "Is that …? What the hell?"

That's when I noticed it, too. A long incision all the way across his neck, blood running from the wound and pooling on the ground.

"You two don't need to look at this," he said, bending down to try and scoop up me and Mum simultaneously.

But I wasn't going anywhere, and Mum's eyes were transfixed, her breathing still ragged. Then I realised she wasn't looking at our cat.

"Mum?"

I followed her gaze to see what she was staring at. What had happened to Loki had been only half the reason for the scream. The other part was even more sinister. A piece of paper was lying beside his body, bloody fingerprints marking the edges. On it were written just five words.

Animals should not be caged

Chapter 24

Date: March 14th
Followers: 10011

SORRY FOR STOPPING SO ABRUPTLY EARLIER, but just reliving it all got to me. It's hard to believe he's gone. I can hardly remember a life without Loki. He's just been there with me for so long. When I was on chemo he would curl up on my lap and sleep for hours, like being with me was his favourite place to be. When I got better he used to sit on the armchair in my room and listen to me practise drums. I'm not sure how I'm supposed to be okay without him. It's 2 a.m. now, and I can't get to sleep, so I figured I'd try and bring you up to date.

In the aftermath of finding Loki, everything

descended into chaos. Mum looked so white, I thought she was going to pass out.

"Stay here. Whoever did this can't have gone far. You call the police. I'll go look," Noah said, then darted off to perform a lap around the house.

"I'll grab some torches," Glen added.

Dad appeared, took stock of the situation and went back inside again, only to return a few moments later armed with the weapons from his study: an ancient crossbow and one of those terrifying balls on a chain with spikes coming out of it.

Noah ran up panting.

"Nothing," he said.

Glen handed out the torches and the three men headed out, waving them around. I ran up to Dad.

"You need me with you," I hissed. "You know I'm stronger and faster than the rest of you. Besides, I can see in the dark."

"Which is why I need you to stay with your mother," he muttered. "She'll be safe with you."

I turned back to find Mum was trying to get Loki into a shoe box. Her heartbeat was all over the place.

"Here, let me," I said and took the box from her. I started to gently lift him to put him inside. But something was off. The blood wasn't clotting. It continued to flow from the wound and the cardboard was soaked red before he was even in it. I pushed the thought to the side for the moment and put the lid on.

"They'll find whoever did this to him," I said, trying to coax her to speak, but she could barely lift her eyes to look at me.

Every part of her was trembling. Knees, hands, shoulders. Then, in an instant, she changed. I have no clue what caused it, but she was suddenly standing upright, hands on hips.

"We should be looking, too," she said.

To be honest, although she was on her feet, she didn't look in a fit state to go anywhere. Her hands were still shaking, and her eyes were darting around erratically. I tried to say as diplomatically as possible that this might not be the best idea, but my mother is not one to be told what to do.

"If there's anyone still out there," I said, "Dad and the boys will find them."

"They've gone over to the west side of the farm. But there's the back barn near the woodland. They won't think to check there."

"Then we'll tell them to do that when they get back. Or I can sprint over there if that would make you feel better."

She shook her head, emphatically.

"We should both go. We need to stick together."

And just like that, she was striding off into the dark, not even bothering to get herself a coat first. When we reached the barn, she stopped and looked at me.

"Can you hear anything in there?" she asked, nodding towards the old building.

I listened closely, the still night making it very easy.

"Rats and mice. That's about it."

"Nothing bigger?"

"Bigger, like a person?"

"Anything bigger. Moving."

I shook my head. I would have loved to know what was going on in her head as we stood there, because her heart was skipping all over the place, but that was nothing compared to the smell of adrenaline that was pouring from her.

"We should go in and check it out anyway," she said, her hands clenched into tight fists at her side.

"Mum, I promise you, no one is hiding inside."

"I need to see for myself," she insisted.

As I've mentioned before, I don't go out around the farm, and I was actually surprised at the condition of the barn. It had clearly been patched up at some point, and all the walls were in fairly good repair The door, however, wasn't. It hung open. And there, glinting on the ground, in a shaft of moonlight, presumably coming from a hole in the roof, I spotted the brass owl paperweight that I got for my seventh birthday.

Now, you maybe or may not know, depending if you read the earlier posts in this blog, that on a particularly rough day, I threw said paperweight out of my bedroom window. But given how upset Mum already looked, it didn't seem like the right time to tell her that.

"Come on, we need to head back. If we're not there when the others return, they'll worry."

I took her arm and led her towards the house.

"There was no sign of anyone," Noah said, as I fixed them all drinks—triple measures. "No car and no tracks that we could make out. It's like they vanished into the night. And I don't get how they could have been that close to the house without one of us hearing or seeing something. Ryn and I were sat right outside, for goodness' sake. It doesn't make sense."

"No," I said, trying to disguise how shaky I was feeling. "It doesn't."

"I still think we should call the police," he added.

"There's no point," Dad said, still holding the spikey ball thing. "They won't come out tonight over a cat. I'll go into town tomorrow and see them. They won't be able to ignore me that way."

"Are you sure you're all right, Mum?" Glen asked. "You're really pale. Maybe you should go have a lie down?"

"You'd think being a doctor I'd be used to the sight of blood," she replied, attempting to laugh, but the sound caught in her throat and none of us was able to reciprocate. "Actually, I'm going to take Loki down to the lab and clean him up before we bury him."

She went outside and fetched the cardboard box that

was still dripping and marched down the steps to the cellar.

"Is she okay?" Noah asked, with a look that implied he thought she was a raving lunatic.

"It's best we leave her to it," I said. "To be honest, it'd probably be best if you go now, too."

A crease formed between his eyebrows as he contemplated how to answer this.

"I don't feel right leaving. You could be in danger."

"Trust me. We'll be okay."

He didn't look convinced.

"Look, you guys searched the grounds, and I would hear if someone was outside."

"What are you, a bat?" he said, before shaking the comment away. "Sorry, I just wish you'd call the police straight away."

"Honestly, Dad's right. They wouldn't do anything tonight."

Without saying any more, he moved away from where Dad and Glen were deep in conversation, and I knew he was after some privacy. Obligingly, I followed him outside.

"I don't mean to sound dramatic or anything, but I've already admitted to waiting nine years to get to this second date. I don't think I could bear it if anything happened to you. Please, I'll stay on the sofa. I'll sleep in my car, even, but I'd rather I was closer to you."

Sure, I've had a fair few romantic moments in my life

before—Fin could turn it up when he wanted to—but there was something about that one. About him offering to sleep in his car to protect me. I do think of myself as a feminist, and let's face it, I'm the last person in the world who needs protecting, but a warm feeling spread through me, which only intensified when he lifted his hand and placed his palm against my cheek. I shifted towards him, pressing my chest against his chest. A small involuntarily groan escaped my mouth as his thumb brushed against my lips. So little of our skin was touching and yet it was doing everything to me. Honestly, it felt like his pulse was mine and I was alive again. Our eyes locked, his hands now on the small of my back pulling my hips into his. And I knew exactly what he was going to do. He was going to kiss me. And I wanted him to. Scrap that. I needed him to. I closed my eyes, waiting for our lips to meet. But my mother's voice cut through the moment.

"Merrewyn, Glen, can you come into the kitchen please," she called.

The disappointment that hit me in the stomach was matched perfectly by the look of agony that twisted Noah's face at the near miss of our first proper kiss. With an apologetic smile, I took his hand and squeezed it. (At human strength level.)

"I'd better go. I'll see if she's okay with you staying on the sofa. Otherwise, it might have to be your car."

"As long as I'm close to you, I don't care."

Another moment passed between us. Another second

when I was sure we were about to have our first kiss, when Mum yelled again.

"Merrewyn!"

She was standing in the kitchen, Glen and Dad propped up against the table. Her pulse had settled by a fraction, but I have no idea how, because her adrenaline was at an all-time high.

"Glen, there are some suitcases in the back store-room," she said. "Can you dig them out? We'll have to travel light."

"Suitcases?" Glen began to object.

"We need to go. We all need to leave, right now."

"Mum, don't be ridiculous. You heard them. Whoever it was has gone."

"I just tested Loki's blood. There's venom in it."

I didn't need to ask for clarification as to what that meant. None of us did. A stunned silence descended on the room. I was the one who finally broke it.

"He was killed by a vampire," I said.

"Which is why we need to get going now," she insisted.

As she moved to pass me, I grabbed her by the elbow.

"You go, but I'm staying," I said.

"What?"

"I don't want to go anywhere."

Now I know what you're probably thinking. Yes, this vampire is most likely the murderous one from the bowling alley the other night, and I'll admit that was not ideal. But it's another freaking vampire!! If I could just get close enough to have a conversation with it, maybe it would know of others it could introduce me to. Other, hopefully less murderous ones.

"You cannot be serious, Merrewyn. This is a vampire we're talking about."

"I know, but what's it going to do, kill me?"

"This is not a joke."

Dropping the humour, I tried again, this time attempting to appeal to her more rational side.

"I know what you're saying Mum, and if you want to go, then go. I completely get it. You need to keep safe, but if it had wanted to kill any of us, surely it would have done so earlier? What was stopping it?"

"I don't know, but I'm not sticking around to find out. I'm getting you all out of here now."

"Where? Where do you plan on going that's safer? I mean it. It's a vampire. It can smell us. It'll just track us down if that what it wants."

She was even paler now than she had been earlier, and that's saying something.

"Well what do you think we should do?" she asked.

That came as a shock, believe me. Sure, my mum asks my opinions on small things in life, like what she should get Glen for Christmas or whether or not her boots go with the dress she's wearing. But never on big, life-changing things like what to do if you believe there might be a dangerous rogue vampire on your heels. Given the severity of the situation and the surprise of the question, it took me a minute to answer.

"Dad," I said, turning to him. "You're the expert on these things. What should we do?"

And, at that point, I'm afraid I'm gonna have to leave you in suspense for a bit as my brain is a bit fried. I'll update the blog later today.

Chapter 25

Date: March 14th
Followers: 10438

MORNING FOLKS, so let's pick up where we left off yesterday.

It turns out my dad is a little more resourceful than any of us had realised.

"Just to clarify," I said, as we looked up at the UV strip lights that run discreetly around the house under the gutter, "you put those up there to keep me prisoner here?"

"It was a precaution I took when your mother was away and you were having one of your big sleeps," he said all matter of fact, like it was totally normal.

"And you didn't think to mention it to me?" Mum cut in.

"I didn't think we'd ever need them."

"Do they even work?" I asked.

"Go inside," he said, pulling out a remote.

I did as I was told and watched from the doorway. Dad pressed a button on the small black controller but nothing seemed to happen.

"I think they're on," he said.

"Wonderful," Mum muttered, not trying to hide her disdain. "Merrewyn, put your hand out the door."

"What?" I cocked my head to the side. "You want me to put it under there?"

"Only for a second. You can be quick about it."

Obviously, I wasn't a major fan of this plan, but however bad I felt beforehand, it wasn't a patch on how I felt afterwards. As soon as my hand passed the door-frame, a flash of heat seared my skin. Snatching it back, I examined the red patches on my knuckles and fingers. To be fair, it wasn't much worse than a touch of severe instant sunburn but more than a second longer would have caused considerable damage.

"Fuck, Mum."

"It works then," she said to Dad, then lifted herself up onto tiptoes to give him a peck on the cheek. "Smarter than you look, Dr Colt."

The irony of Mum congratulating my father on having developed a system to keep me trapped at home, when she was the one always trying to get me to leave it, wasn't lost on me, but I couldn't see any point in bringing it up. It's not like they normally listen to me.

"Well, what about Noah. Isn't he going to think it's a bit strange?" I asked.

He was currently with Glen, sorting out the guest room. Trust me, we laugh at that title. *Guest room.* Like we have ever had anyone to stay. Mainly, it's used as an extension of Dad's office with all sorts of boxes piled in there, but there is a single bed hidden in the corner, and while I'd been talking to Mum and Dad, the boys had been getting it ready.

"Noah won't know they're there as long as he doesn't go outside," Mum said. "Although I really don't know why you didn't tell him to leave."

"I tried, but apparently he's as persistent as the killer vampire that's following me."

"What do you mean, following you?" she demanded.

At that point, I thought I'd blown it. I didn't want to tell them about the deaths at the bowling alley and get Glen into trouble for hacking the police records, but more importantly, I didn't want Mum to get any more stressed than she already was. The cortisol pumping through her body was so strong it was dizzying. Besides, it sounds ridiculous, and I can't explain it properly, but I knew we weren't in any danger. I still don't think we are. I don't know how I know this, but I can feel it in my gut. Sure, whoever killed Loki is obviously deranged, but there were four humans around at the time who the vampire could have easily taken out, particularly given the boost they'd just had from their massive feed on Craig and his girlfriend. So why didn't they kill any of my family? Well the only reason I can think of is that they didn't want to. They're about more than just blood and murder. Still, I couldn't say any of this to Mum, so instead I shrugged it off the best I could.

"I mean, it's come to our house, hasn't it? It's come to the home of a vampire. It clearly knows I'm here. That's all I'm saying."

She eyed me sceptically, before sighing and nodding in agreement.

"You're probably right," she said.

Sensing that the conversation had come to natural pause, and not wanting it to suddenly restart, I made my excuses to leave.

"I should go check on Noah," I said, bolting for the stairs before Mum could stop me or call me back, although even she's had to accept that selective hearing in vampires in very real.

Upstairs, Noah and Glen were chatting away with grave faces.

"I'll leave you two to it," Glen said, when he saw me in the doorway. Then he looked at Noah. "I'm just down the hall if you need anything."

"Thanks. I'll be good."

And then it was just the pair of us, together.

Now before I get into this, I want to address what more that one of you have said in the comments. I get it. Noah being the vampire looks like a fairly reasonable conclusion to jump to, IF you ignore one obvious fact. HE HAS A HEARTBEAT! Seriously!!! Come on guys. You think I wouldn't notice if the bloke I was dating was dead? Have a little more faith in me.

That said, I will admit that something's unnerved me about the attack on Loki, apart from losing him obviously, that is. I didn't smell anything. Not a thing. I mean, I know I don't give off a scent. (It's the whole microbes and teeth-cleaning thing again.) But I'd never thought about if this is true where other vampires are concerned and the fact that it wouldn't be possible for me to smell them at all. I'll admit that is slightly scary. But I don't want to think about it right now. I want to talk about Noah.

"Are you all right?" he asked, crossing the room and placing his hands on my hips the moment Glen left. That felt good. His hands there. His presence in the house. "I really wish your folks would let me call the police."

"Mum has persuaded Dad to call them now," I lied flawlessly. "I'm sure it's just some local farm kid, a little psycho who has graduated from burning ants with a magnifying glass."

"And is able to run off at the speed of an Olympic athlete?" Noah added sceptically.

"Can we talk about something else?" I said, plonking down on the bed.

He followed suit. Sitting so close our knees were touching.

"Okay, how about deciding where we're going for our next date?"

"Our next date?" I said, coyly.

"Yup. Date number three."

"Number three? You're counting this as number two?"

I acted appalled by this suggestion, despite the fact that before we discovered Loki, playing cards outside had been the most fun I could remember having in ages. Besides bowling, that is.

"Well, I'm not anticipating these ending any time soon, so if you want another number two, I suppose I can stretch to it, but I have to admit, I was looking forward to date number three."

"You were? Why's that?"

"Well, you know what they say about the third date ..."

Jesus, you have no idea what the sexual tension was like in the room at that moment. I mean, I've experienced it before. Fin and I had every intention of going all the way, before I died, but this was different. This was like with every breath he took it was harder and harder for him not to rip his clothes off. And I was no better. Obviously my pulse wasn't racing because I don't have one, but my skin felt as if it was on fire. And not like when I tested Dad's security system. It was like electric sparks were buzzing through me. A static charge that was drawing me towards him.

"Can I kiss you?" he whispered.

His breath against my skin felt like an invisible touch that I craved would explore my whole being.

"You can definitely kiss me," I said.

And that was the start of it. My first kiss with Noah. I don't know how long we were kissing for. A minute? Ten minutes? An hour? Who knows? Eventually his lips left mine and traced their way over down my neck towards my collarbone. I pressed my body closer to his, fighting the urge to throw all my inhibitions aside.

"I am never letting you go," he murmured as he pulled my top over my head and resumed kissing my neck before slowly edging down. His other hand slid down my back and into the top of my jeans, his fingers toyed with the waistband of my underwear. My own hands were gripping his hips, pulling him into me. Over-come by desire a deep animalistic growl escaped from within me.

And that, ladies and gentlemen, is what brought an end to this potentially X-rated encounter. In case you didn't read that properly, maybe caught up in the moment as we were, I'll repeat the last bit for you again, all in caps.

I released a DEEP ANIMALISTIC GROWL.

Not a *grrrr* you're so sexy growl. Not a Tony the Tiger you're *grrrrr-eat* growl. I growled like a freaking wild animal when you get between it and its food.

One moment we were kissing with such force it was taking all my strength not to tear the T-shirt straight off him and push him down onto the bed. And the next I was leaping to the far side of the room at near vampire speed.

"What is it?" he asked, with a look of bewilderment on his face.

I had one arm outstretched, as if to keep him at a distance and the other across my chest. The fact was, that sound I'd emitted had reminded me my instincts were perhaps more animal than human. I was dangerous and could hurt him. And all this was moving way, way too fast.

"I think we need to slow things down," I said. "A lot."

"I get it."

He stepped towards me, his arms out now, too, like he was approaching a cornered dog. In one hand he held my top. My breaths were ragged. My desire to dig my nails into his skin still overwhelming. Slowly, he handed me my top. Gradually, my fear ebbed away and I lowered my arm.

"I'm sorry," he said, now right beside me. "I'm sorry if I pushed things."

"It wasn't you."

"It was. I was the one making jokes about the third date and everything. I'm just crazy about you. I … I can't explain it. I really can't. And I know it's stupid, ridiculously soon, but they always say that when you know, you know, don't they? And that's what it feels like, I feel like, with you. I know this is how my life is meant to be. But I get that's waaaay too much pressure on you. So I'm just going to back up here and pretend I never said anything."

His cheeks were flushed in this super cute way as he looked up at me from under his eyelashes, that irresistible grin sneaking back onto his face. As much as I tried, I couldn't help but grin back at him.

"I need to go and check on Mum and Dad," I said. "Maybe you need to take a cold shower."

He raised his eyebrows.

"From the way you were kissing me back, I don't think it's just me who needs one of those," he smirked.

At which point I turned on my heel and left to go to bed.

Chapter 26

Date: June 3rd
Followers: 12812

I DON'T KNOW why I thought I'd be ready to do this today. I don't know how I thought I'd ever be ready to do it again. Before I sat down at the computer, I had so many things in my head that I needed to tell you. But now I'm here, I can't even manage to type his name …

I guess stuff like this takes longer to recover from than I thought.

Thanks to those of you still here and those still messaging. But I'm not sure when I'll be able to face writing about what happened next, if ever. It just doesn't seem real. It doesn't seem possible that he's gone. That I'm never going to see him again.

I'm sorry. I can't do it. I'll try again another time. I promise I will try.

Chapter 27

Date: July 7th
Followers: 13241

HEY ALL, so I'm back. Or at least I'm going to try to be, and I need you to bear with me, because this is seriously freaking tough. But I know I need to do this. I promised myself I would. You deserve the truth and closure, just like I did. So here goes.

It's been nearly four months since my last proper post. Four months since everything tumbled out of control, since I found that threat next to my murdered cat and discovered someone was hunting me down. Finally, I'm at a place—physically, mentally, geographically, you name it—where I feel like I can talk about what went on. It's still not easy. I still find myself overcome with emotions: rage, anger, sadness, all the time, but I know that some of you have been worried, and I feel like you have a right to know. (And some of you are dicks who can just piss off, but I don't have time to care about idiots anymore.) To be honest, I don't think I'll ever be 100% ready to share everything that happened, but if I don't make a start, I'll run away from it indefinitely, and I need to move forward with my life.

I guess I should do a quick catch up of where we were in the last post, for me as much as you. I had to skim back so I could remember where I got to. Just reading about it made me feel sick all over again. Reading about him in those earlier posts.

If you remember, the people at the bowling alley had been murdered a couple of days before I discovered Loki dead with the note next to him. Mum was seriously freaked out, and I was little bit concerned, but mostly I was excited. Firstly, because I'd never met another vampire and secondly, because of that kiss in the bedroom with Noah. Even now, I find myself thinking about it. About Noah's hands exploring my body. His lips on my skin. The way he made me feel. In that moment, life had felt as if it was moving in the right direction for once. How fucking wrong I was.

That night I wasn't the only one who didn't manage

much sleep, and it was just before dawn when Noah started stirring in the guest room. Knowing that Mum and Dad were likely to put a ban on me seeing him until we'd got to the root of the vampire issue and desperate for a repeat of the previous night, I pushed opened his door by a fraction.

"Hey, you," he smiled from the bed.

His hair was tousled and his face lined with creases from his pillow.

"Hey, yourself," I said.

During the next fifteen seconds, all I wanted was for some hidden vampy sense to kick in and let me read his mind. I was desperate to know what was going on inside his head. Crazily so, but then again, I reckon I could read most of it from the glint in his eyes.

"So …" he said.

"So …"

I sat down next to him and combed my fingers through his hair. Pretty brazenly if I'm honest.

"Careful, there's only so many cold showers I can have here without your family thinking something's wrong."

I laughed as he pushed himself up to sitting position and kissed me again. It was different to the night before. Weird how I remember that, right? So many things have happened since. So many life-changing things, and even with my enhanced memory, I'm sure I've forgotten some of them, but those kisses, God, I recall them so clearly and how tender the moment was. There was none of the previous desperation, but that was OK. It felt like we had years ahead of us to keep kissing.

"What are your plans today?" he asked. "Your dad's still going to the police station, isn't he? Are you going with him?"

For a second I thought he was joking.

"You know I can't leave the house in daylight, right?"

"Sorry," he blinked, shaking his head. "I … I forgot. It's just things feel so natural with you. So normal, you know?"

"Yeah, well normal is something I am definitely not."

Despite my morose response, he grinned.

"Well, I think normal is overrated," he said, at which point I knew exactly what was coming. This time I instigated it, although I discovered it's hard to kiss someone when your cheeks are aching to smile.

"Come on," I said. "Mum and Dad are pretty stressed. It's probably best if you get off soon."

"I understand. But I can see you again, can't I? Tonight, maybe?"

As I stood up, I couldn't help but laugh.

"Have you ever heard the expression *playing it cool*?" I asked.

"Why on earth would I want to do that? I'm crazy about you. Have I not made that obvious already? Unless you'd find me more attractive playing it cool, in which case I can definitely try. Is that what you'd like?"

Yup, that morning I laughed as I pulled him up from the bed, taking care not to dislocate his shoulders. Now, I'll be honest, I wasn't exactly ogling him, but it is fair to say there may have been a bit of absent-minded staring at his smooth, toned chest and that thin line of fuzzy hair that disappeared into his boxers. You can't really blame me.

"I'll be down when I'm dressed, unless you want to stay here and help me?"

"What did we just say about playing it cool?"

"You're right. Get out of here. I don't want you seeing me looking hot and dishevelled."

Thinking back now on that moment, it's still hard not to smile. Maybe it's just because I'd gone without company for so long, but I couldn't recall ever meeting someone who'd made me laugh quite so much as Noah did.

Downstairs, and the rest of the family were stirring, too.

"Merrewyn, you need to drink," my mother said, the moment I stepped foot in the kitchen. "You haven't had a proper one for days now."

Part of me considered objecting, given how conscious I was of our limited supply. But with everything going on the last thing I wanted to do was put Noah and my family at any more at risk. So, after a quick listen to ensure Noah was still getting dressed upstairs, I grabbed the cup Mum handed me, popped in a metal straw and took a long suck. When I pulled my mouth away, I gasped in satisfaction. Until that moment, I hadn't realised quite how long it had been or the effect that was having on me. In the end, I finished the entire cup, although afterwards I wasn't sure whether that had been the wisest decision.

A couple of minutes later and Glen was downstairs.

His eyes went straight to me.

"Good night?" he asked, innocently.

"Perfect," I replied.

"A sleepover at twenty-four, how about that?"

"Shut up," I said, unable to control a grin, although it vanished almost immediately when he turned to Mum and Dad.

"Anything get caught in the lights?" he asked.

They shook their heads, obviously disappointed.

"So, what's the plan now?" he said. "I still have to get to school. I've got a mock chemistry exam today, and I seriously need to ace it."

"Your father and I discussed this last night. We think you still attending school is a good idea, for now at least," Mum said. "Plus, I need to go to the surgery to show my face and pick up some stuff. When I get back, I'll do a full necropsy on Loki, see if there's something I missed. But I want you to pack a bag before you leave. Your father and I will be making a decision later about whether or not we're staying. Personally, I don't think it's safe here. Not at all."

At this point, she shot my father a look which made it more than apparent that they had opposing views on the matter.

"Maybe here *is* the safest place to be," I said.

They all looked at me. Now, as you're probably aware, my family don't normally turn to me for advice. On anything at all. On medical issues we defer to Mum. For paranormal and vampire issues, we have Dad. (Yup, I'm not the expert even there) And for anything else, we have Glen. Which was why it was so unusual to have them looking at me, waiting to hear what I had to say.

"Well, think about it," I continued, as I quickly tried to create a rationale for what I'd just said. "If you were a vampire, chances are a populated area is a much better bet than a place where there's only one house in a four-mile radius. Ours is also probably the only one set up to repel them. And there's no reason to assume my presence carries an extra risk. I don't have a scent, meaning they might not even know another vampire lives here. The more I think about it, the surer I am that last night was just random dumb luck."

None of them replied to this, which I took as a good sign. They're normally pretty damn quick to shut me down when they think I've got it wrong.

"Right, well if that's the plan, I guess you'd all better

get on with things," I said, hoping I might be able to sneak another half an hour alone with Noah before he left. As I should have guessed though, things never work out the way I hope.

More on that tomorrow.

Chapter 28

Date: July 8th
Followers: 13848

AFTER MUM AND GLEN LEFT, Dad retreated to his study to paw through some books for anything useful on tracking vampires. Only once everyone was out of the way did Noah come downstairs. I suspect it was a deliberate delaying tactic on his part, so he could avoid any awkward conversations, and I can't say I blame him. Sadly, when he appeared, he was fully dressed.

"So would it be wrong of me to assume that you don't have plans for tonight?" he asked.

"Why, did you have something in mind?"

"I thought we could grab a takeaway and watch a film. Or head to the cinema if you like."

It's strange the way he spoke to me then. Like I was just some normal girl he was causally dating. As if our lives weren't about to implode on themselves. Like I wasn't … you know, dead. For a split second, I allowed a vision to form in my mind. Noah and me, just a normal couple, doing normal-couple things. Perhaps, if this continued, he and I could attend Lovisa's wedding together. (Only the reception, obviously. I don't think hoodies are a good look at wedding ceremonies, and let's be honest, they're my go to for daytime wear.) But before I could reply, Glen came marching back into the kitchen with a face like thunder and a pulse that was double its normal rate.

"Where's Dad?" he snapped.

"In his office sorting out something. Why?"

"My bloody car won't start, that's why. How long have I been saying this was going to happen? And I can't afford a further non-attendance. Not after last week. I need him to give me a lift and I need to leave now!"

(It's a shame because I feel like, in lots of these posts, I make him out to be kind of moody and stuff, but honestly, he's not. He is genuinely the sweetest person that you could ever have in your life, and that's coming from his big sister, so it must be true. But at this particular point in time, he was definitely stressed and that can make him act like a bit of a douche.)

"Well, I can take you," Noah said, casually.

Glen stopped in his tracks.

"You can?"

"Sure. Colchester, right? That's where I'm heading anyway. I'm doing a mural at the Miserable Mermaid fish and chip shop there."

"The Miserable Mermaid?" I said, sceptically. "That can't really be right. Why on earth would a place call itself that?"

While I was quite interested in the marketing reasons behind what was definitely a crappy name, Glen was not in the mood for listening.

"Can you go now?" he asked, ignoring me. "I really need to leave straight away."

"No problem."

Noah reached into his pocket for his keys and threw them to Glen.

"Put your stuff in the car. I just need to kiss your sister goodbye."

Yup, that's what he said. And the way I've written it makes him sound really arrogant. But it wasn't like that at all. It was really sweet. The emphasis on the word *need,* like he couldn't possibly leave without kissing me. The second Glen disappeared, Noah turned back to me.

"So, is that all right? Can I kiss you goodbye?"

He took a step towards me and a fluttering, that felt very much as if my heart was beating, started in my chest.

"Well, you've already told Glen that's what you're going to do," I said, teasingly.

"You're quite right, I did. And I'm a man of my word."

"So, in that case, I guess you'd better kiss me."

It was strange. In that moment, I felt like I was having an out-of-body experience, watching us kissing as a spectator. Everything about it felt so right. The pace of the kiss. The closeness of his body to mine. Even though I was aware that only a few feet away from him was a fridge full of blood bags, it really couldn't have been any better. Far too soon, though, he broke away.

"I better not keep Glen waiting," he said. "But I can see you this evening?"

"As long as you don't think you're going to come across as over eager," I said. "You know, a girl could find that off-putting."

As I struggled to stop myself grinning, he was at the door, blowing me a kiss.

Now if comments were switched on, I'd probably have a hundred of you messaging me in caps lock, asking why the hell I'd invite him back to a house where my cat had been murdered the night before, and I will admit, it probably wasn't the brightest idea, but thank God I did. I dread to think what would have happened if I hadn't.

Anyway, I'll get to all that. I heard the car door slam shut before the engine started and the car sped off down the driveaway. And just like that, he was gone.

Given that I couldn't remember the last time I'd had a shower (remember, no sweating or microbes, so it's not that gross), I was about to head upstairs to the bathroom, when Dad appeared. His glasses were perched on the end of his nose, making him look like some wise old owl, and he scratched at his temple for a good ten seconds before he spoke.

"Merrewyn. Can you come into my office, please? There's something we need to discuss."

Given that my mind had been entirely on Noah and the shock on Dad's face when Glen had talked about Noah and me having a sleepover, I seriously thought I was about to have to face the *birds and bees* talk. A massive lump wedged itself way up in my throat, forcing me to swallow it back down before I spoke.

"Actually, Dad, I was about to go and have a shower. Tidy my room a bit."

"That can wait," he said, with a firmness that he generally never shows. "This can't. Come with me, please."

So that was it. I followed him into his study. And what he had to say was damn near crazy.

Chapter 29

Date: July 9th
Followers: 14022

I KNOW these posts are coming more slowly than they were before, but one a day is all you're going to get at the moment, I'm afraid. It's not that I'm lacking time. I've actually got more on my hands than I would have anticipated in my current situation. But I spend a lot of it trying to block out everything that's happened. Rehashing it doesn't let me do that. So, like I said, one post a day from now on.

Yesterday, I mentioned in my post that my dad was pretty insistent that I go and talk to him in his office, and despite how much I don't like the place, I knew I couldn't refuse. When I was young, I viewed his office as a cavern full of mystery and intrigue, of ancient artefacts and intriguing tomes; now, every time I step inside, I'm mostly concerned about catching something from thousand-year-old scripts. Honestly, those things probably house more pathogens than a service-station toilet brush. I know it's ridiculous. You can guarantee that, wherever I am in the world, I'm almost certainly the deadliest thing within a hundred-mile radius, but those old papers make me shudder. What can I say? Sometimes fears are irrational, even when you're dead.

"Come and sit down," Dad said, beckoning me in from behind his desk

The only seats in the room were covered with books and papers, but seeing that he had his hand held out waiting, I figured I should try to get comfy and—despite my aforementioned phobia—went to relocate a pile of dusty-looking manuscripts. He jumped up like a shot.

"No, no, no. Not like that. Here, let me. I'll do it."

He then spent the next five minutes picking up each sheet of paper separately and then placing it carefully on top of a mammoth and precarious pile on his desk. If I'd have known how long it was going to take, I would have probably come back later, but at least I wasn't the one having to touch them.

"So," he said, when we were both finally sitting down.

Despite my improved reflexes and senses, time moves at a normal pace for me, but in that room, at that moment, it felt as if I'd slipped into a vortex, because as you may have gathered, finding the right place to start a conversation was difficult for my dad at the best of times, and at that point, it seemed almost impossible. I watched his chest rise and fall with several deep intakes of breath before he finally fixed his eyes on me with any form of certainty.

"I want you to know that everything I told you before about vampires hunting in packs or murdering for … for pleasure … well, I'm still absolutely certain that it's true. Or at least, it always used to be."

I could feel the *but* hovering in the air between us. I did him a favour by voicing it.

"But …?"

He hesitated.

"I know your mother doesn't believe in all this *mumbo jumbo,* as she likes to put it, and she has her experiments to back up her findings—and, my goodness, we would have struggled without those—but we do have to factor in the limitations of such experiments and take the science of the supernatural into consideration, also."

"Science of the supernatural?"

"Yes."

He scratched his head, an act I reciprocated. So far, I had no idea where the conversation was leading or what the point of me being there was. I cast my eyes around the room and waited for him to get to the point.

"So," he said, eventually, after clearing his throat half-a-dozen times. "I guess we should get started."

"Started?"

"On seeing if these things work. Your mother is not the only one who can do experiments."

I closed my eyes and rubbed my temples.

"Sorry, Dad, you've lost me. What experiments are we doing?"

"Yes that's good. Just keep your eyes closed."

"What?" I said, my eyes automatically pinging open.

"No, no. If you could just close your eyes again?"

"Close my eyes?"

"Just for a second."

I frowned and considered saying no, because honestly, at that moment, I had absolutely no idea what was going on. But as is often the case with my dad, it's sometimes easier not to question. I sighed to myself and shut my eyes again.

A cold liquid suddenly splashed all over my face, and I instinctively opened my eyes.

"What the hell was that?"

"Holy water. From the fonts of the Vatican. Blessed by the Pope himself," Dad said, excitedly.

"And you just threw it at me?"

I was having a hard time keeping myself seated in the chair at this point.

"In the name of science. How do you feel?" he asked me.

"Mad," I replied.

"Great, great."

He shuffled his papers around to find a pen and started writing in a random notebook.

"Any burning? Blistering?"

"Only on the inside."

It took him a second to realise I wasn't talking literally. His face fell.

"I have to admit, I had high hopes for that one," he said, letting out a long sigh before picking up a small bottle and throwing it across into his office bin with impressive accuracy. "Clearly not worth the money. Okay, how about this one? Hold out your hand."

I hesitated.

"Is this one meant to burn my skin off as well?"

"Quite possibly, but as the last one didn't work, I'm not feeling too optimistic. But at least I got this one at a discount."

I looked at what he was holding: a small red stone about the size of a two-pound coin.

"What is it?" I asked, nervously.

He grinned. He'd obviously been waiting for that question.

"The Heart Infernal," he told me. "Formed from the blood of a siren."

I grimaced.

"Are you sure you don't want to have a tranquilliser handy, in case I turn?"

He stopped and stared at the stone in his hand. His brow wrinkled into a set of lines.

"I don't think so. You don't plan on biting me do you? You can always drop it if it starts to hurt."

"Fine," I said. "Give it here."

I have to admit, there was a small, perhaps masochistic, part of me that was almost wishing this one would do something. Maybe it would singe a hole through my palm or instantly desiccate me—only a little bit, obviously. Deep down, I hoped that this mystical stone did hold a power against other vampires—the bad ones—should I have to encounter them. I held my breath and reached out my hand.

"Anything?" he asked, after a minute of silence.

"It feels a bit, damp," I offered, helpfully.

"Well, I most certainly overpaid for that one too, then, despite the discount."

He took the stone back, and it went the same way as the bottle of holy water. I scanned across his messy desk for his next failure.

"Anything else?" I asked.

His lips pursed and his head tilted towards the door, despite the fact that we were the only people in the house.

"Only one thing, but this is a bit different."

His tongue flicked out from his mouth and he drew it along his dry lips. A moment later, he opened his desk drawer and pulled out an antique-looking gun.

"Jesus, Dad!" I yelled, lurching back in my chair.

He put it down in front of him although honestly, that didn't really help me relax. Given that I considered him to be the staunchest pacifist I have ever known, seeing this weapon lying casually between us was more than a little surprising.

"A gun? You want to give me a gun?"

"This one was built in the 1880s by a Polish monk, specifically for killing vampires."

I looked a little more closely. It had an ornate handle with a pattern carved into the dark wood and a fairly conventional-looking trigger. Beyond that, it barely resembled any other gun I'd ever seen. The barrel was open along the top, creating a kind of trough, and there were two spring devices, one on each side. On the tip of the barrel was a metal circle with a cross mounted on top, presumably to act as a sight.

"Are you sure it's all there?" I asked.

He ignored my jibe and continued.

"Originally, the bullets, or rather stakes, were made of hardwood, but these," he said, pulling out a smooth cylindrical metal object about the size of an expensive cigar from the drawer, "are slightly more modern. Built from a diamond-based alloy, they are near enough the hardest objects on earth. You won't manage to blunt one of these or break it for that matter, meaning they're entirely reusable, assuming of course you ever manage to retrieve one after it's been fired. Ideally, you would go straight for the head, but a shot to the heart or even a leg should manage to slow them down for at least a little while."

He picked up the weapon and carefully laid the futuristic-looking stake in the barrel. There was a light click as it settled into place. He pointed it towards a rare spot on the wall that didn't have papers or pictures pinned to it and squeezed the trigger. The gun bucked in his hand and the stake shot upwards and embedded itself just below the ceiling.

I stared at him, open-mouthed.

"Quite a kick there. You might want to get a little practice in first," he said and pulled out a wooden box with a dozen or so more stakes in it.

I paused, and a deep silence fell on the room.

"Take it, please. It will help keep you safe."

"I can look after myself. I'm a vampire remember?"

He held my gaze, and in that moment, he didn't look like my dad at all. He suddenly seemed old, frail and full of worry. A chill drifted through the room, causing me to shudder. I hesitated a second longer, before I managed to speak.

"Fine. I'll take it."

He smiled at me as he handed it over.

"Also, could you be a dear and pull that out?" he said, indicating the stake he'd just shot into the wall. "Your mother will go mad if she sees it."

Chapter 30

Date: July 10th
Followers: 14621

I'M TEMPTED to turn the comments on again. It's kind of weird not having them. It almost feels like I'm talking to an empty room. But I know if I do, I'd be faced with a barrage of questions that I'm just not in a position to deal with right now. Maybe when I'm finished. Perhaps when I've got to the end of this, if I'm still sane, I'll open them up to you guys then. When it's over, trust me, you'll be as lost for words as I was.

Based on tests Mum has done on the rats and me, it's clear the brain and central nervous system play an important part in a vampire's ability to function. Therefore, destroying the brain or severing the spinal cord is almost certainly enough to take a vampire down.

What about the heart? I'm sure you would be asking.

Given how prevalent the stake-through-the-heart is in all vampire lore, literature and movies, you could be forgiven for assuming this was an obvious method of dispatching one of my kind. But all of my mother's research seems to suggest that it's not a sure-fire kill. After all, it isn't beating in the first place. It's clear that the heart is the only vital organ aside from the brain that a vampire has (something to do with processing the blood we absorb), but given time, and assuming it hasn't been totally destroyed, it could, theoretically, heal once the stake has been removed. So, a shot to the head or severing it from the body, is the best way to end a vampire, which is why I slathered myself in sunscreen and whacked on a hoodie and jeans for a bit of target practice outside.

I could have made the trip to the forest in a tenth of the time, less maybe, if I'd wanted to, but I didn't. Despite the tingle from the sun, I walked slowly through the fields, lost in my thoughts. My dad was scared. Genuinely scared. It was an emotion I'd seen in him before, during every hospital visit when we'd have an appointment with the specialist and my cancer would be discussed in sombre tones. But this was different. Whether I thought I needed a gun didn't matter. He needed me to have one.

I'd planned on going straight into the trees, to benefit from the shade and use one of them as a target, but upon reaching the barn—you know, the one where my paperweight went through the roof—I had to stop. There was something about the place that drew me out of my thoughts and commanded my attention. Something was emanating from the space that made my skin prickle even more. I took a step towards it, intending to go inside but changed my mind and shook my limbs to try and free them of the sensation. I was being ridiculous, just remembering Mum's fear and confusion there the night before. That was what I thought, anyway. I brushed the feeling aside and carried on.

Reaching the woods, I walked deep into the shade. I pulled out one of the metal stakes and used it to etch a smiley face into a broad trunk. (I even added some fangs, which thinking about it now, was a little perverse.) I would like to say I was as natural with a gun as I was with a bowling ball, but shooting requires skill, not brute strength. The first hurdle was sliding the ammunition in, not as easy as Dad had made it look, not to mention that the trigger was stiff. I could see now why he'd fired so erratically before.

After an hour, I'd managed to get the hang of loading and firing, although getting it to go where I aimed was another matter. The sight, which I realised might actually be more of a religious motif, did little to aid my accuracy. At one point, I considered that maybe vampires are genetically predisposed *not* to use guns, although I dismissed that theory when I finally hit my smiley vampire square in the eye. After that, I started to get into the swing of it and pretty soon was hitting two out of every three.

What *was* slowing things down was the need to read and reply to Noah's texts. (Yes, I know what I said about typing faster than average, but it still takes you out of the swing of things if you're constantly stopping and starting. And it was pretty constant.) The messages were just about general stuff—letting me know that he'd dropped Glen off and that he was at the chip shop finishing his painting. Telling me how much he was looking forward to seeing me again. Despite the interruptions, there was something comforting about the ease with which we were communicating. Like we had been doing it for years. However, as I said, they always seemed to arrive exactly as I was about to fire off a shot. So, the sixth time it happened, I sent him a quick *See you later* message and turned my phone off.

Just before midday, when the prickling of my skin was starting to really bug me, I was surprised to see Mum's car trundling down the driveway. Whilst her coming back so soon was a surprise, the scent that accompanied her was even more of a shock.

I gathered up the stakes and headed back to the house where I found her unloading a cooler box from the boot of the car.

"What's this?" I asked.

"The local rugby club had a donation session this weekend. I completely forgot. It was the last one I booked in. Luckily, the nurses were on hand to make sure everything went smoothly."

I popped the lid to find two dozen blood bags inside.

"Mum! You can't take so much in one go. Someone will spot it's missing."

"Of course they won't. They'll just assume there was a logging mistake. Now come on. Have another drink. You've be rationing yourself for a fortnight now. You need to get your strength up."

I wish I could have seen it now. I wish I could have read through all the fear that was clouding her eyes and causing her heart to skip, but here's the kicker: it's tough to recognise when people are lying to you when it's what they've been doing your entire life.

As I reached into the box and pulled out a bag, she smiled broadly. And for once, I didn't even bother with a straw, just sank my teeth straight into the plastic. One gulp later, and I was feeling on top of the world.

"You've got to love a vegan," I said, with a grin.

Chapter 31

Date: July 12th
Followers: 14624

SORRY I DIDN'T post yesterday. I know I said I'd do one a day, but a lot of things are happening in my life at the minute, and I needed to clear up some life admin. Believe me, that's a sentence I never thought I'd write, but so much has changed in the last four months. Maybe when I get to the end of this, I'll be able to tell you a bit more about my life now. Where I'm living and what I'm up to. Or perhaps it would be better to just draw a line under the whole thing. To put the previous chapter of my life to bed once and for all. We'll have to wait and see, I guess.

Now, back to the story. I had just downed a couple of

substantial gulps of blood and was feeling great. Honestly, being out in the sun, even when almost one hundred percent covered, can take it out of you. Thankfully, as I said before, blood from a vegan really charges you up, and my good mood lasted for a solid five minutes. That was how long it took until I saw the newspaper that Mum had brought back with her. The front page had a follow-up story on the *wild-dog* attack at the bowling alley. It's wrong to say I'd forgotten about Craig and his girlfriend. I really hadn't. But I'd let it slip to the back of my mind, and there it was again, staring me right in the face.

I read the article, learning more about them, how they'd both been accepted at their first-choice universities to study drama and graphic design but were taking a gap year, first. It seems they'd been together since they started secondary school but had been friends since the first day of primary school. My heart was aching, possibly from the massive volume of blood I'd just consumed but more likely because of what I was reading and the guilt that came with it. I was spending my time thinking about Noah and reliving our first kisses, while Craig would never get to kiss the girl he loved ever again. Which is why I felt I had to do something. I couldn't just sit around and read or watch Netflix. I needed to be taking action. I needed to know who this vampire was. I needed to find them.

Now, one feature I don't think I've told you about before is vampire memory. It's awesome. Seriously amazing. From what Mum's test have shown, the brains of the vampire rats don't appear that much different from those of the normal ones, except that they're firing far more quickly. I'm sure you've heard people talk about how we only use ten percent of our brain, right? Well, that's bullshit. Yup, I'm sorry, but it is. You can Google the science on that one for yourselves. And I know there are loads of films based on that concept—some good, some less so— but it's fiction, so yeah, please don't go around spreading stuff like that. Anyway, the difference between you and me isn't how much I use, it's how rapidly I'm using it. Every second, every single neurone in my brain is firing at a rate of nearly 100 Hz, which is over four times the average for a human. That's where the super speed, super strength and night vision come from, according to her. And it's why I have a nearly eidetic memory, too (or photographic memory if you prefer). I'm basically a superhuman. A dead superhuman.

(I'm not telling you this to gloat or boast, by the way, just to explain that even though I'd never actually broken into a police database myself, I'd seen Glen do it countless times, and well, you know, *monkey see, monkey do*.)

I can't tell you exactly what I was thinking at the time. It just felt like the only way I could help. Maybe I imagined that if I could track down this vampire, I'd be able to talk to it and persuade it there was another way to survive that didn't involve killing people. Or maybe I just couldn't stand being useless anymore. It didn't matter. I had a plan.

The first problem I encountered when I entered Glen's bedroom was that he'd left the curtains wide open. Generally speaking, we are a closed-curtain house, for obvious reasons, but that day, his were drawn wide apart and bright sunlight was cutting right across the room. Normally, I wouldn't dare go into such a situation without full body covering and sunscreen on, but I had fixated on this one idea. So I did what vampires do so well and raced to the window, grabbed a curtain and whipped it across before doing the same to the other one. It was definitely the quickest I'd done anything like that before, and the blood I'd just had meant the headache was minimal, but that didn't stop my arms from blistering into angry red boils. Biting down on my lip, I ignored the pain and got to work with the task at hand.

Fortunately, I know all of Glen's passwords to everything. I have done for the last year or so, since he shifted from little brother to probably my best friend on the world stage. Not that I'd ever tell him that. Anyway, while he takes his laptop to school, his desktop was sitting there like it was just waiting for me, and within a minute, his computer screen was alive, and I was on my first page of the dark web, ready to do my first solo hacking job.

I'll be honest, I wasn't entirely sure what I was doing or what the lines of code I was typing meant, but I just called up my memories of when I'd seen him doing it before and typed it all in exactly the same. And what do you know? It worked! Well, the first part, at least. I was into the National Police Data Base. But where did I go from there? Then I thought about what I'd said to Mum about a vampire stalking me. If that really had been the case, then there was only one other place I'd been where it could have done that. Lovisa's engagement party.

Turns out, there's a lot of crime logged in London, even on a Wednesday night. Graffiti, joy riding, burglaries. Lots of burglaries. No murders though, which I took as a really good thing. I was only checking one day, but the fact there hadn't been any killings in that area of the capital, helped ease my mind a little. But did that mean a vampire hadn't been stalking me? Was it a local to this area only?

I'd have to try another angle. I thought about what else it was that Glen used to look at, and a couple of minutes later, my screen was lit up with all the hospital records of the twenty-four hours surrounding Lovisa's party. If I'd thought the police had a lot to do on a Wednesday night, this site was off the charts. Endless admissions, from broken noses in punch ups, to emergency appendectomies and heart attacks.

However, one particular record caught my eye.

Unexplained death.

I clicked on the cell to expand the contents within it. And just like that, the floor fell away from my feet.

Chapter 32

Date: July 13th
Followers: 16249

SORRY TO LEAVE you on a cliff hanger yesterday. My phone started ringing. I could lie and say I got lost in a deep-and-meaningful conversation and that's the reason the post looked half finished, but it wouldn't be true. It just distracted me. I didn't even answer. It was my mother. She calls multiple times a day to try and speak to me and it feels good to let her know I'm deliberately ignoring her. I should probably just turn the damn thing off or throw it in the bin. After what she's put me through, I'm not going to change my mind and let her back into my life.

Anyway, I was telling you about hacking into the hospital database and finding that on the night of Lovisa's engagement party there'd been a death - in her very building. One in which the only immediate signs of injury were two tiny puncture marks on the side of the elderly lady's neck and an unknown toxin in her blood.

Yup, a vampire had killed an old woman in Lovisa's apartment building at the same time as I was there. Loki, Craig and Co and now this. As far as I was aware, there were only two common denominators joining the three events. Me and Noah.

I know you guys suggested this before, and I'd dismissed it, but at this point, I didn't believe he could be a vampire. He had a heartbeat and an aroma, and he could go out in the sun. But I knew that I wasn't the killer, and like all good detectives in novels, I was starting to believe less and less in coincidence. Noah might not be a vampire, but I was certain he knew something about what was going on. Maybe he was working with one. Perhaps some have a *familiar* or an *acolyte,* or whatever you want to call it.

"Glen!"

The next thought that crossed my mind sent me leaping up. I'd sent my baby brother off in a car with Noah that very morning. Perhaps he'd been using our dates as an opportunity to scope out potential feeds for this vampire he was working with. Perhaps that was the reason he stayed at our house overnight, so he could be there when the vampire came back for its real meal after Loki. My family! I raced to my room, picked up my phone and started calling Glen, repeatedly. Each time, it rang out.

"Fuck! Fuck!"

I paced around, trying to work out what the hell I could do. He might not be answering because he was in class, but then it might be because Noah had killed him and taken him to his vampire master. With a flash of inspiration, I quickly opened a search page on my phone. I wasn't able to reach Glen, but I was hopeful that if could track Noah down, that could lead me to him.

Jabbing at my screen so hard a crack appeared, I typed in *The Miserable Mermaid*. I scrolled down. There was a Blue Mermaid chip shop and a Mermaid restaurant, but neither of them were in Colchester nor had *Miserable* in their name. Of course. It was fake. He'd been making everything up. He'd been playing me for a fool this entire time. With a sinking feeling of dread settling in my gut, another thought sprang to mind, and after a further quick search, I found what I was looking for and hit the call button.

"Colchester Boys' College," said a lady with a strong Essex accent. "How can I help you?"

I cleared my throat, unable to stop myself from shaking.

"My brother, Glen Colt, I need to know if he made it into school today."

"Glen Colt?"

"Yes. He's in the sixth form. Can you tell me? Can you tell me if he's there?"

I could hear tapping.

"Yes, Glen has been in since first period registration. Is there a message you'd like me to pass on to him?"

"No," I said, as relief flooded through me, only to change my mind a second later. "Actually, yes. Can you tell him to ring his sister, please? Tell him to ring Merrewyn?"

"I will get that message to him."

"As soon as he's out of class, please. I need him to do it right away."

"I understand. Is there anything else I can help you with?"

I hung up without bothering to offer a reply. Glen was safe. That meant Noah hadn't done anything to him, yet.

Now by this point, I hadn't completely given up the ghost on this blog. And as I needed a bloody big distraction to keep me sane while waiting for Glen to call me back, I thought I'd get on it quickly. It's safe to say that was massive mistake.

In case you haven't seen, a lot of guys on here jumped straight to the Noah conclusion well before me, and my whole inbox was bursting with messages.

- *He went back into the bowling alley to talk to Craig, right? And then Craig ended up dead. Seriously, how much more obvious do you want the clues to get?*

- *Did he turn the lights off in the bowling alley for you, or for someone else?*

- *There's something not right about Noah. You need to be careful around him. I don't trust him.*

I wish these were the only ones, but honestly, there were hundreds like it. I mean it. Hundreds. After fifteen minutes, I slammed the laptop shut and tried to get a hold of my thoughts, but they were spiralling away. It seemed so obvious now that Noah had to be involved, but why? Was it revenge for leaving his brother the way I did, or maybe it was my fault for ignoring him as a kid? That was what I thought. Maybe the whole thing about Fin and him not really talking was a lie. Maybe Fin had actually put him up to this, to hurt me as much as possible.

But then that would also mean he had to know I was a vampire, and if that were the case, then surely he was taking a huge risk being alone with me so often, not to mention kissing me. It didn't make sense. None of it make sense.

I took a deep breath and shook my head clear. I was being ridiculous, panicking. Only a couple of days before, some of you had been filling up the comments section accusing me of murdering Craig and his girlfriend. I knew you were wrong then, so why was I suddenly convinced you were right now? I really don't know. All I can tell you is that I was feeling desperate and confused and didn't know what to think.

That afternoon was long. Seriously long. I spent the entire time staring at my phone, waiting for Glen to call. Given that it was just past two when I rang the school, I figured I'd hear from him within about ninety minutes, as soon as classes ended. But three thirty came and went, and still there was nothing. Perhaps he'd run out of battery, I thought, but then my calls would have gone straight to voice mail, rather than ringing out. And if he'd left his phone a home, I'd have been able to hear it here, even if it was under a pile of clothes.

More than once, I got the gun out, assessing its weight and running my fingers across the barrel like I was actually considering using it. Were the stakes really capable of killing someone like me? I wondered. It seemed unlikely, given Dad's track record with the holy water and the stone, but maybe I'd have no other option.

By four thirty, I was a total wreck. I couldn't stop moving. I was going to have to speak to Mum. I went downstairs, telling myself to play it cool.

"Has Glen texted you today?" I asked her, as nonchalantly as possible.

"I don't think so," she said, not looking up from her work. "My phone's just over there."

She nodded to the small table next to her easy chair.

I hurriedly moved across and grabbed it. Zero messages or missed calls or anything else that would be helpful to me.

"Well, did he tell you how he was getting home? He hasn't got his car, remember."

She finally looked up.

"From what you said, I assumed he was getting another lift with Noah. Didn't he say he was coming back here after work? And if not, I'm sure he'll message if he needs picking up. But, since we're talking about Noah, we should—"

"Stop talking!" I snapped.

Mum's mouth clamped shut, her eyes widening in surprise at the tone of my voice, but I couldn't speak. I was listening, and this time I actually heard it: the sound of a car rumbling up the driveway. I strained to locate the heartbeats beneath the noise of the engine, or to pick up any scrap of conversation, but there was nothing.

"Merrewyn!" Mum called after me, as I dashed away.

I yanked open the front door and took the steps in one leap, ignoring the rays of the afternoon sun as they singed my skin. The car was approaching the house now. Noah's car. And inside was Noah. On his own.

Chapter 33

Date: July 14th
Followers: 17244

I'M HAVING to ration blood more than ever before, these days. Every sip I have leaves me worrying about how much I've got left and how long that's going to do me for. But last night, the thirst got too much, and I allowed myself a decent drink. I don't know if it was the right thing to do, but I've been struggling to concentrate properly on meagre amounts, so I treated myself. Anyway, it'll hopefully make it easier for me to get through the rest of the story for you. Or at least another good chunk of it.

When Noah arrived back at the house without Glen, my instinct was to rip his throat out. I'm not joking. I wanted to pin him to a chair and make him bleed. But I needed to know where Glen was first. Then I'd make him suffer. That was the plan.

"Where's Glen?" I demanded, as he walked up to me, then shifted away from him as he went to kiss me on the lips. "Was he not coming back with you?"

"I thought so. We agreed that I'd pick him up. But I guess his plans changed. I waited for nearly thirty minutes, then figured he'd just got a mate to drop him home, instead. Is he not here yet?"

You need to remember that I was stressed. Seriously stressed. All I could think about was my baby brother ending up the same way as bowling-alley Craig, and every part of me was certain that Noah was the one responsible.

"No, and he doesn't go anywhere without letting us know where he is. And he doesn't get lifts back here, either. Ever. And Mum and Dad don't like visitors."

At this point, Noah realised that something in our relationship had drastically shifted. He tilted his head to the side and viewed me, quizzically.

"Ryn, what am I missing here? What's wrong?"

"I just want to know where my brother is."

"Okay. Well, have you tried calling him?"

"Of course I've tried calling him. He's not picking up."

"Right. Then we'll have to track his phone."

"Track it?"

"Sure. You're all on the same network plan, aren't you?"

I nodded.

"It'll be easy enough to find him, then. Here, pass me yours, and I'll show you."

I was a hundred percent certain that this was a trap, and he was going to spring something on me. But by this point, I also assumed he knew what I was and that I would be ready for anything he might try. So I pulled my phone out of my back pocket and held it out to him.

He took it without a word, tapped the screen and swiped across it several times.

"Here you go," he said, showing me an app I'd never seen before. "That's Glen's number, right?"

I nodded.

"Well, according to this, his phone is twenty-five metres away from us."

I shook my head.

"It's not. I've be calling it all day. I would have heard it."

"Maybe it's buried down the back of a sofa or something."

"I still would have heard it," I insisted.

Despite my less-than-friendly tone, he walked indoors, still holding onto my mobile, and stopped in the hall. I followed him like a school kid on a scavenger hunt.

"That's odd," he said. "We're further away now."

"Give that here," I barked, snatching it from him and

heading back outside, where the reading started to drop again.

A few paces later and it was down to five metres, then three, then one, and I was standing right beside Noah's car. I opened the passenger door and there, in the footwell, was Glen's phone. I picked it up and opened it. Over twenty missed calls and all from me.

"What the hell is it doing here?"

Noah shrugged.

"I guess he must have dropped it."

"No, Glen's not careless like that. He knows how important it is for us to keep in contact."

"So, what are you saying? That I took it from him?"

Maybe I should have played my cards closer to my chest, but the fact is, by this point, I really didn't feel like I had any cards at all. I was missing Glen. And people were dying.

"Where were you today?" I demanded.

"What do you mean? I told you. I was painting a mural at the Miserable Mermaid."

"It doesn't even exist!" I burst out, so loud that a flock of birds took to the sky from the barn on the far side of the field. "Don't you dare lie to me!"

"I swear I'm not, Ryn. What is the matter? Are you okay? Let's go back inside."

By this time, my shouting had brought Mum and Dad out of the house.

"Merrewyn! What's going on?"

"Glen's missing! He's missing and his phone was in Noah's car."

"Glen's missing?" My mother paled. "No, he can't be."

"He is. I rang school. He turned up there this morning, and I asked them to pass a message to him to call me back, and he hasn't. His phone was in Noah's car. Somethings wrong. I can feel it. Something is very wrong."

Noah stepped forwards, his hand out like he was going to comfort me, only to change his mind and drop it again.

"Okay," he said, using a slow, calm voice. "You're obviously upset, but there's got to be a simple answer to this. Where is he likely to be? He's got a boyfriend, hasn't he? Can we call him? And we can check bars and other places around his college."

Now this was actually very sensible. It was the logical thing to do. But I wasn't thinking logically. The rugby-team blood I'd drunk had been full of testosterone and, combined with the fact that I was working entirely in vampire-brain mode, meant I was not behaving rationally. Think angry toddler, absolutely impossible to reason with, then add super strength and fangs. Something I'd kept hidden from Noah. Until then.

I moved so fast that even Mum and Dad didn't see it coming. Grabbing him by the throat, I spun around, flew across the drive and pushed him up against the wall of the house, his feet dangling a foot off the ground.

"Merrewyn!" Mum yelled, racing to my side and

trying to pull me off him. "This is not helping. This is not helping at all."

I didn't even care that my fangs were out. And they were. Gleaming and dripping with venom.

"He knows! He knows what's happened to Glen! Just like he knows what happened to Loki and Craig and his girlfriend! He knows! He knows!"

Noah's eyes were locked on my fangs. I could feel his pulse quickening beneath my grip, as he wheezed through his constricted windpipe.

"Merrewyn! Let him go!"

"Not until I have answers!" I screamed back.

My Dad was tugging at me now, shouting at Mum to get a tranquilliser, and for a second, I thought that was what she was going to do, but instead, she dropped her hands and looked at me.

"You need to let him go, Merrewyn. He's not the one who has the answers. I am."

Chapter 34

Date: July 15th
Followers: 18236

I USED to think there was nothing that dreadful about lying. In fact, I believed it was sometimes necessary. Inevitable, even. I'd seen it could have benefits. Just small white lies, like answering *Yes* when a friend asks *Do you like my dress*? Or telling someone you enjoyed the food when you're over at their house for dinner. What harm could lies like that possible do? If anything, surely they make the world a kinder place. But they don't stay small, I learned. They tend to grow and develop a life of their own that swells and feeds off their surroundings, until they end up so complex, so entwined you can't remember where the truth ended, and the lie started. And it all goes wrong. Even when you had the best intentions.

"What do you mean, you have the answers?" I said.

My fangs remained out, glistening, but my grip on Noah had loosened by a fraction. Enough to allow him to breathe a little easier.

"What did you find out? You know who did it?"

I don't think I'll ever forget the way she looked at me in that moment. The sadness that filled her eyes as she rested one hand on my shoulder and slowly drew my arm down with the other, lowering Noah to the ground.

"We should go inside. You need to sit down to hear this."

"We have to find Glen, first."

"I know. I know we do, darling. And we will, but I need to tell you something now."

Her hand was still squeezing my shoulder, trying to reach past the vampire part of me that had taken over, to calm me. I could hear the rush of her blood and smell the stench of her fight-or-flight adrenaline. But she wasn't fighting me or running away. She was just standing there, staring at me with such sorrowful eyes that I couldn't look away. And that had been her plan.

Normally, my reflexes are exceedingly sharp, but this situation was anything but normal and while I did catch a flash of the syringe at the last moment, it was too late. Her aim was swift and accurate.

A second later, I hit the ground.

Chapter 35

Date: July 16th
Followers: 18776

I HAVE TO APOLOGISE. I know I said I was going to make these posts longer, but that last one … well, it was unexpectedly hard to relive all the things that happened then, especially the way I attacked Noah. Thinking about everything I learned that day, I know the rest I'm going to share with you will be even more difficult. But I'm ready for it today. So, sorry. I'll try to get back on track now.

If I was to hazard a guess at what you're thinking at this point (or go and check my messages), it would be somewhere along the lines of *Why on earth would your mum shooting you in the neck with a tranquilliser be tough for you when you've pretty much spent this entire blog describing all the countless times she's done it before*? And I get it, but the thing is, all the other times she tranqued me, I'd needed it. I was on the edge. I was dangerous. But right then, I wasn't. Sure, I may have pinned Noah up against the wall and gripped his neck a fraction too hard, but I had things under control. I was talking to them, for crying out loud. All I wanted to do was find Glen, but instead, the world went black.

When I came to, I was sitting in a chair in our kitchen. The curtains were drawn, as normal, but I could tell that it was dark outside and knew that at least a couple of hours must have passed since Mum jabbed me. The second thing that struck me was how unusual it was for me to wake up downstairs, as my parents always carry me up to my bedroom to let me sleep it off. And the third, was Noah's presence.

"You're awake," he said.

He was standing the other side of the kitchen with a knife in his hand. The tip quivered as the trembling of his hand spread along the blade. Now, I have to give credit where credit is due. When I was human, had someone with fangs attacked me, I'm pretty sure I wouldn't be standing there waiting for them to wake up, even if I was armed. Not to mention the bit about my own mother sedating me. It's not exactly normal third-date stuff, is it? Part of me is still amazed he didn't stab me while I was still out of it, but that wasn't on my mind right then.

"Where are my parents? Where did they go?" I tried to stand up, but the effects of the drug hadn't subsided completely. I wobbled, and Noah darted across the room, dropping the knife onto the counter as he came. When he reached me, he grabbed my shoulders and lowered me back into the chair.

"You need to take it slow. What can I get you?" he asked, as I tried to steady myself.

"How long have they been gone?" I tried again. "I need to go after them. I need ..."

I clutched my head. Normally I'd give myself a couples of hours to come round properly after sedation. I might listen to some music or put the TV on quietly in the background. But there was no time for that.

"You can't go anywhere like this," he said. "You can barely stand."

"In the fridge," I pointed, conceding that he was probably right. "Grab me a bag from the top shelf."

With his back to me, it was impossible to see his reaction as he opened the door and saw what was inside, but his heart stuttered, skipping a full beat before returning back to a steady, if quickened, pace.

"Is this what you mean?" he said, handing me one of the bags. "Do you need anything else? A glass? A straw?"

Rather than reply, I just sank my teeth straight in

through the plastic and gulped down the contents. Gradually, the dizziness subsided. Though that meant it became harder to ignore the way he was staring at me. He was obviously trying his hardest to stop from gaping.

"So, you really are a …"

His voice drifted into the ether as if he couldn't bring himself to say the actual word. So I said it for him.

"A vampire. Yup. Mythical creature sitting here in the kitchen."

"Okay." He drew a deep breath in. "So, the photosensitivity—"

"Is technically true. I can't go out in sunlight. Not unless I've got an extreme amount of sun block on."

I was ready to go into the full spiel, like I had with Lovisa, and was preparing myself for all the questions that would ensue—just like with you guys, when you asked about things like my soul and super strength and how I was first turned—when I remembered the urgency of the situation.

"How long have they been gone?" I said again. "What time is it?"

A glance at the kitchen clock allowed me to answer my own questions. It was nearly 2 a.m., which meant they'd been gone nearly eight hours.

Another eight hours of Glen in the company of a vampire that clearly had blood-lust issues. The blood in my stomach curdled.

"We need to go now. Straight away."

I sprang up again, this time managing to stay on my feet, if still a little unsteady. I grabbed another two blood bags from the fridge and immediately started on one of them.

"Did they say where they were going?" I asked. "Did Mum say anything else?"

"No, she just kept apologising to me. Then told me and your dad to stay with you. Said it was her mess and she'd fix it."

"Shit! Shit!"

I thumped the table, not realising the force I was using. The wood splintered and it split in two.

"Okay, that answers my question about super strength," he said, taking a step backwards.

"So where's Dad?"

"He chased after her and jumped into the car. Yelled at me to stay with you and told me where to find the syringes to put you out again if I was worried." His voice lowered a fraction. "That's what you've had to go through? Them stabbing you with a needle any time they get worried?"

"We don't have time to talk about that. I need to know where they've gone. And what the hell does she mean it's her fault? How can it be?"

Noah's heart continued to hammer away at twice it's normal speed, although he was thinking more rationally than me. Or at least, it seemed that way when he then suggested the most sensible solution."

"Ring them," he said. "It has to be worth a try."

I will admit, I felt a little bit foolish for putting my fist through the kitchen table in frustration, without even stopping to think of something as logical as calling my parents to find out where they were. I grabbed my phone from the dresser and dialled Mum's number. I was expecting it to ring out, the way it had all those times when I'd tried to get through to Glen. But it was answered almost immediately. But not by Mum … or Dad.

"Hello Merrewyn, I've been waiting for your call."

Chapter 36

Date: July 17th
Followers: 19576

NOAH DROVE THAT NIGHT. He didn't need me to tell him what to do, or whether I wanted him to come with me. The second I hung up the phone, he had his keys out, ready to go. We'd just reached the car when I remembered something.

"Hold on a second," I said.

I darted back into the house returning a moment later with a leather case and a small wooden box.

"What's that?" he asked, as I climbed in.

I unzipped the case and showed him the gun. He didn't comment, just started driving. In fact, he didn't say anything at all until we were on the main road, two or three miles from the house.

"So, who was it?" he said. "And are you sure it's the person who's got Glen, too?"

"I don't know, but he said he was at the Castle with my family," I replied.

"And you really have no idea who it is?"

"I don't …"

I'd been racking my brain ever since I'd heard the voice, trying to place it. The hoarse, gravelly tone could have been any villain in a film, but something about it resonated with me, like I'd heard it before. But where?

"Maybe it's the vampire who turned me," I hazarded a guess. "Or one that's come across my blog and wants to shut me up."

"You have a vampire blog?"

"It's fairly new. It seemed like a good idea at the time, but now …"

Noah was driving considerably faster than the speed limit, but it still didn't feel fast enough. More than once, I thought about getting out and sprinting there, but that would use up energy I was desperately trying to replenish, and although I didn't know much about this vampire, it was clear he'd had at least three full bodies worth of blood in the last week. As Mum—and the incident involving me biting Glen once—had proved, the energy gained by getting it directly from a human is much greater than from a blood bag.

"Is that how much you need to have?" Noah asked, watching as I drained the third bag.

I wiped my mouth with the back of my hand.

"Not normally, but I need all I can get. Whoever this vampire is, he's been drinking directly from humans, which means he's going to be faster and stronger than me. I'd hazard a guess that he hasn't been pumped full of sedatives recently either."

"Wow. I guess I should be glad to hear you haven't been drinking from humans?" He tried to add a light chuckle, but I couldn't reciprocate, and he quickly dropped his attempt at a smile. "It's going to be fine, Ryn. Your family are okay. He told you that much. You're going to get there and put your fist through him, the same way you did that table."

It was sweet of him to be so encouraging, particularly after what I'd put him through, and I wanted to believe he was right. But I knew in my gut that it was going to go badly.

"Colchester Castle, right?"

"That's what he said."

"Any idea why he'd choose there?"

"None at all. Maybe he's ancient and it was his home once. Honestly, I don't have a clue."

Noah was quiet for a while, but it was clear he was struggling even more with the silence than handling the things I was telling him.

"How will you get in? I mean, I'm pretty sure it'll be

all locked up at this time of night. There'll probably be security, too. You might need someone to let you in."

"I don't need to worry about that, trust me. I'll get myself in, one way or another." I hadn't realised how threatening that comment might sound. His eyes flashed with fear. "I just mean I'm fast. And strong. They won't see me," I said, a little bit offended that he thought I was just going to take someone out.

Mind you, if it had been the only way to get to my family, I probably would have. Once again, we fell silent. It stretched out longer and longer, to the point where I wondered if he was ever going to speak again. Finally, though, as a series of traffic lights turned green ahead of us, he did.

"I don't like it, Ryn. This person is drawing you in. It feels like a trap."

"Maybe he just wants to talk."

"People who want to talk use the phone. They don't murder your cat and abduct your family. Please, think about this carefully. Maybe you should take your time, formulate a proper plan. At least get your strength back."

I'd heard my father's voice in the background over the phone. He'd shouted that they were all okay. That was the word he used, *okay.* I knew it was just a euphemism for alive.

"If I don't go now, he could start picking them off, one by one," I said. "He might have already started. Fuck! Fuck!"

I slammed my fist against the dashboard with such force I'm amazed the airbag didn't burst out.

"What the hell are you playing at?"

The question was aimed at my mother, not Noah, who seemed to understand. I just couldn't imagine what she could have done to get us into this situation. But I did know that storming off like she'd done had made things a whole lot worse. This rogue vampire had gone from having one of my family as a hostage to three, and it was all down to her.

"Would he really be that much stronger, than you?" Noah asked, with quiet concern.

"Yes. Maybe. I don't know. I would think so. I mean, if he is the one who killed Craig and his girlfriend at the bowling alley, then I'd say definitely."

"What?"

The car swerved as his attention snapped to me. Thank god there were no other vehicles on the road right then. But when he'd regained control, the look of shock remained.

"Craig? At the bowling alley? You're not serious. You can't be."

His pale face was full of genuine anguish at the loss of someone he'd hardly known.

"I'm sorry. I thought you would have realised."

He shook his head.

"No. I hadn't."

The silence was different this time. I could sense his

mind whirring as questions formed there. But I was definitely not expecting what he said next.

"Could you feed from me?"

"Sorry?"

I was sure I must have heard him incorrectly. But when he repeated what he'd said, there was no room for misinterpretation.

"Could you feed from me? This vampire, you said he's stronger because he's been using live humans rather than blood bags, right?"

"Yes, most probably."

"Then you're already on a back foot and that's without considering the fact that you've been unconscious for the last eight hours. Wouldn't my blood help even up the odds?"

I didn't even stop to consider his suggestion.

"No," I said, immediately. "I don't do that."

"Why not? I'm offering."

"It's not that simple. It … it could be difficult to stop. Maybe it wouldn't be for experienced vampires but it definitely would for ones like me, who haven't had the practice."

We hit a set of traffic lights that turned red just as we reached them. Noah took the moment to look me straight in the eye.

"I trust you," he said. "I think you should use me."

Chapter 37

Date: July 18th
Followers: 20165

ISN'T it strange how the passage of time is often subjective? Sometimes a single moment can feel as if it's stretching out for hours, and yet another time, an hour can feel like it's gone in a heartbeat. That car journey seemed to be taking an eternity. As the city came closer, with more houses emerging along the road, each second was agony. My mind whirred constantly as I tried to make sense of the situation and failed. What could my mother possibly have to do with the killings and Glen being taken? Had something gone wrong with one of her experiments? That was the only thing I could come up with. But she'd been so certain that the rats couldn't transfer the condition to humans. And it's not like they ever came into contact with anyone outside our household, anyway. But what else could it possibly be?

The man's voice echoed around my skull as I tried to think beyond my paranoia and work out why it seemed so familiar to me. Vampire memory—obviously not quite as perfect as I'd thought. Trust me, though, I'm never going to forget it now.

As we reached the outskirts of the city, brown tourist signs directing us towards the Castle appeared by the roadside, and we followed them. Until we didn't.

We reached a roundabout, but rather than taking the turning indicated, Noah skipped straight past it and took the next one.

"Wait! What are you doing? You're going the wrong way."

"It's fine. I know a quicker one."

His eyes were fixed on the road, but I didn't need to see his face to know he wasn't telling me the truth.

"You're lying to me. What's going on?"

"Trust me. This is for the best."

"Turn back! Turn back right now!"

I went to grab the steering wheel, but another car was coming the other way.

"Please, Ryn, just trust me," he said.

The thing is, I didn't. He'd seen what I was. I'd attacked him and he'd watched me drink blood, too. He'd stayed with me when I was unconscious and could have left. He had just learned that vampires were real, yet he was so calm. It was too good to be true how well he was handling it all.

"I swear, if you don't turn around now," I said, in a low voice, "I will grab the steering wheel, and I don't care who I hurt in the process."

I wasn't lying. In that moment, I would have done it, regardless of what happened to us. But as I went to carry out my threat, I saw a new road sign and then a mammoth building with a large car park at the front. Confusion flooded my thoughts.

"Noah, what are we doing at the hospital? Why are we here?"

He remained staring forwards, and he was swallowing so rapidly, I could hear the saliva moving down his throat.

"It's less than a two-mile run from here to the Castle. You'll have more than enough energy for that once you've taken what you need from me."

And that's when I finally understood what he was doing.

"No. No. I can't do that. You don't know what you're saying."

"I do, Ryn. I get it. You're a vampire, and vampires need human blood. I understand. So, just leave me enough that the doctors can fix me up again, and you'll be ready to face whatever you find."

I couldn't believe what I was hearing. A searing pain, bordering on agony, spread up from my chest. Something I don't think I'd ever felt before. Tears were pricking my eyes, threatening my precious water supply.

"I told you. It's not that simple. I don't do this. Last time … I could go too far. I could … kill you."

"And I told you I trust you. You won't."

I couldn't speak.

"I've waited nine years for you, Merrewyn. *Nine years* to be with you. The way I figure it, this is just a bump in what's going to be an amazing and very long relationship. Not to mention an awesome story to tell the grandkids."

"Vampires can't have children," I said, although I don't know why it seemed important to clear that up right then.

He smiled sadly.

"Then I guess we'll just have to adopt. We've got years and years to work it out."

The bright lights of an ambulance coming into the emergency entrance flashed behind us. I knew we were losing time, but I needed to think. Noah was right. Yes, I felt replenished from the three blood bags I'd drunk, but did I feel strong enough to face a vampire that had drunk three entire humans dry? Possibly four? Maybe even more, but I couldn't let myself think about that, and I didn't have time. Instead I locked my eyes on the part of his throat where his pulse throbbed visibly.

"I'm sorry," I said, and a second later, I lunged.

It was everything I remembered and more. The intensity. The heat. The growing feeling of power.

I could have stayed sitting there, parked in that narrow road behind the hospital, feeling the warmth of Noah's blood as it flooded into me, for a lifetime. The captivating sound of his heartbeat gradually fading just encouraged me to take more. The seconds ticked by, and the longer I sat there, my fangs piercing his skin, the longer I wanted to remain, his life and mine completely entwined. I had fantasised about what my first time with Fin would be like, thinking that sex was the closest two people could ever get. But it wasn't. This was. How could anything possibly be more intimate than a person willingly offering up their life's blood to you?

Only when his heartbeat faded out completely under the noise of my own slurping, did I snap out of it. Gagging at the sight in front of me, I wiped my mouth and sat up. Noah's body drooped limply to the side.

"Oh God, please be okay. Please be okay."

I couldn't hear anything. Not even a faint flutter.

"God, please!"

I pushed open my door and dragged him over to my side of the car, wrenching him out of his seat belt, then heaved him up onto my shoulder. No, that's the wrong word. Heaved is what I would have done if I were normal, but I wasn't. I picked him up as if he weighed no more than a handbag. It was nothing to me. Any doubts that the other vampire would have the upper hand, were gone. I was more powerful than I'd ever been.

I raced towards the hospital.

"Help!" I yelled, sprinting through the doors of A & E and laying him down on the first free trolley I saw. "Please help! He's lost a lot of blood."

A nurse rushed over.

"Call the Consultant," she shouted over her shoulder. "What happened to him? Was he stabbed?"

"He … he …"

I backed away as people swarmed around him.

"Miss," one of them said, turning to me. "You need to tell us everything you can."

My eyes were fastened on Noah. His skin had paled and what little blood he had left continued to ooze from where my teeth had punctured his neck.

"I'm sorry," I said, retreating through the automatic doors and into the ambulance bay. "I can't help you. He needs blood. And anticoagulants. Just give him blood. Lots and lots of blood."

I cast one final glance behind the nurse and saw the trolley disappear through a pair of double doors. Then I fled into the night.

I knew exactly where I was heading.

Chapter 38

Date: July 19th
Followers: 21765

I GUESS I'm getting closer now. Closer to writing about the loss. Closer to telling you what happened. And I don't want to, because I've been living in denial and this will make it real. I know it will. And I'm terrified. Just be patient with me, okay?

My head was all over the place as I raced away from Noah and the hospital, the loaded gun tucked into my belt and spare ammunition in my pocket. Half of me was thinking constantly about what I'd just done, and whether Noah was going to survive. The other half of me was dreading what I was about to face. And what I might have to do.

Impressive metal gates marked the entrance to the Castle grounds, and large yellow lamps cast wide beams of light up onto the stone façade. Despite Dad's profession and the fact we lived so close, I'd only ever visited Colchester Castle twice and both of those were on school trips. He never showed a great deal of interest in things with a clear-cut history, and that was what this place had. Its past was beautifully preserved and displayed in professionally arranged glass cabinets with clear descriptions explaining the significance of each exhibit, in its museum.

Noah had been wrong about one thing—there weren't any security guards. There were, however, lots of security lights, and as I leapt over the metal gates and dashed across the grounds, I couldn't avoid triggering them. As soon as I closed in on the building itself, I could hear them. Three sets of heart beats. Two fast, one slower than I would have expected. Though I couldn't tell whose was whose, it didn't matter. They were alive. I could still save them.

A bridge spanned the dry moat and led to a large arched doorway. Going in that way would be too obvious, so I skirted around the building until I found a side entrance. Mounting the wooden steps, I readied the gun, my arms outstretched.

I put my shoulder to the door and pushed until the lock gave way with a loud clunk.

"Shit," I cursed under my breath.

Honestly, if it hadn't turned out so tragically, I'd probably find it amusing. A vampire behaving like she was a fucking FBI agent in one of those crime shows. But it was the only reference I had on how to act in that type of situation.

Once through the door, I found myself in a corridor which seemed to run alongside where I remembered the main hall area was. Hundreds of years of aromas threatened to overwhelm my senses, but underneath those were some I knew better than any others. My family. I spun around a corner, careful to avoid crashing into any of the displays, my eyes searching the gloom for Glen and my parents. I swung the gun left and right, following my line of sight. But before I had a chance to locate them, a voice came from the shadows.

"You should put that thing down. The last thing I want is for someone to get hurt."

A wave of nausea swept through me as I twisted towards where the sound had come from. But no sooner had I turned my head, than I saw it. On the other side of the hall, a body was slumped in a chair, its head lolling to the side.

"Glen!"

I leapt into the air to reach him, but mid-flight, a

heavy mass slammed into me and I crashed against a wall.

Dust flew up from the brickwork and into my eyes. I swung the gun around, even more wildly than before, but before my vision could clear or I could get a sense of where he was, his voice echoed around me again.

"I asked you to put that thing away."

I could tell he was right in front of me now, and just as I regained my sight, he ripped the gun from my hand and threw it across the floor. He was shrouded in a thick black cloak (that seemed vaguely familiar), with the hood up over his head, not even his eyes visible. Any hope I'd had of Noah's blood making me strong enough to handle my adversary, instantly evaporated. I will say, though, that I truly believe he saved me that night. Had I not fed from him, then who knows how many more of us would have died.

"Glen! Glen!" I tried to shout, but the blow had knocked most of the air from my lungs.

I was panting with shock and fear. Gasping, crying, trying to reconcile the pain that was gripping me. Meanwhile, the figure loomed over me, waiting. His hands were now plunged deep into the pockets of his cloak.

There was no doubt that he was a vampire, but who he was and why he wanted me, I still couldn't fathom. I was about to say as much when my mother's voice cut through my thoughts.

"Merrewyn!"

Standing is kind of a loose term for what my parents were doing at that moment. My mum was propped up against one of the large steel girders that reinforced the building, squeezing my dad's hands as he sagged against her. The scent of blood eddied around them, and both had cuts on their foreheads and lips, with more blood seeping through my dad's shirt.

"What have you done to them!" I screamed, racing over to them.

Several of the glass display cabinets nearby had been smashed, and I wondered what they must have gone through in the hours it took me to get there. Mum put her hands out as if to stop me, yet when I reached her, she collapsed into my arms.

"I'm … so … sorry, Merrewyn. You … shouldn't … have come," she sobbed, ragged heaving breaths punctuating her words. "I … told you … not to come."

"I'll get you out. I'll get you all out of here," I said, my eyes scanning the room as I tried to come up with an escape plan.

The windows were big enough to get a person through, but they were too high off the ground. Going out through the main door would definitely be the best route. Trying to work out how I was going to achieve this, I reached out to my dad, wanting to check how deep the hidden wound was. A fist came out of nowhere and sent me crashing through another of the glass cabinets.

"I think that reunion's been long enough now, don't you?"

For seven years, I hadn't felt any real pain. Nothing other than the occasional blisters from sunlight. I hadn't even thought it was possible for me to do so anymore, but I was learning how wrong I'd been. A searing sensation burst through my side, as if my ribs had been shattered, but I bit down, determined not to show just how bad it was.

"You've got me here," I said, through a clenched jaw. "That's what you wanted. Now let them go."

His face may have been in the shadow of his hood, but I would have bet my immortal life that he was smirking.

"Oh, is that what I want? You seem to think you know me already, Merrewyn. Now, tell me, how might that be?"

Thankfully, the pain was easing, probably due to the crazy volume of Noah's blood flowing through my body. And while I knew I wasn't as strong as him, I was fighting for my family. Which is why I didn't hesitate to push back my shoulders and square up to the monster.

"At least show me your face," I said. "At least let me know who you are and why you're doing this to me."

He paused, the fabric of the hood moving as he tipped his head to the side.

"You're right. How rude of me. I should have introduced myself. My name is Christopher."

Christopher. The name rattled around in my head. I'd gone to school with a Christopher, but this man was too old to be him. Even with my perfect memory, I was still oblivious.

"No?" he asked, noticing my confusion. "Well, that's understandable. We didn't have much time for pleasantries the last time we met. Perhaps you're better with faces than names."

He pushed back his hood, and that was when everything I'd believed about the last five years of my life crumbled away.

Chapter 39

Date: July 21st
Followers: 29655

FIVE YEARS HAD PASSED, but I knew I would never forget that face. It had haunted my nightmares, along with the memory of his limp body dropping to the ground beside Lovisa's car. But I never thought I would see it again.

"You …" was all I could managed to choke out. "You're …you're …"

A smile spread across his face and his cheeks flushed, no doubt thanks to the humans he'd enjoyed over the last week. I could practically feel it radiating from him.

"You can say it, you know. I'm a vampire." The pain

that he'd inflicted was transformed into something else. An agony burning from within my very cells as he continued to speak. "I'm glad you remember me. That's good. Like I said, introductions were somewhat absent last time. In fact, I'm not even sure I got your name. But I managed to pick it up. It's amazing what you can find out when you're given enough time."

"I don't understand. You were fine. You got a blood transfusion."

"Ah. I can see why you're confused. Perhaps this is where you take over the story, Angela. Don't you think?"

The causal way in which he used my mother's name made my skin crawl, but I was still totally baffled. It didn't make sense. The night I'd bitten him outside Fin's house, he'd collapsed, but I'm sure I remembered hearing his heart still beating, even as Mum stabbed me in the neck, and I succumbed to the tranquiliser.

"Come on, Angela. Come and join us. Yes, let's have a proper reunion, shall we?"

I looked at my mother, desperate for some indication of what I was supposed to do, but her eyes were on the ground. And her hesitation cost her.

"I said, come here!"

His voice was a screech, an animalistic scream that rattled the glass of the undamaged display cabinets. Before I could blink, he'd leapt across the chamber, grabbed my mother by the neck and hurled her towards me.

"Mum!"

I jumped forwards and managed to catch her before she hit the floor, although now I was close to her, I could see just how bruised and battered she already was.

"I'm so sorry, Merrewyn," she said, blood dribbling from her mouth.

"You have nothing to be sorry for. Nothing at all."

"Now, that's not technically true, is it Angela?" he said, walking back to us. "Don't be shy. Tell her. I mean I can if you'd prefer. I was never much of a storyteller, but five years locked in a barn can change a person, as I'm sure you can imagine. Although you did visit me from time to time, didn't you, Angela? But then you stopped. And that made me sad."

"I don't understand," I said, clutching at my head.

What kind of horrendous nightmare was I trapped in?

"You don't understand why your mother used to visit me? Well, we had some nice little chats. We talked a bit about you. About you getting sick—and the other thing, of course. We even discussed Colchester Castle. How I'd been here as a child. I'm glad we had that conversation now, of course, otherwise I don't know how your mum would have thought to look for Glenny here. I would have had to think of another plan, I suppose."

"You were locked in a barn? In our barn?"

"Come on, Merrewyn. You're not that slow. Surely you can work this out for yourself."

He was right, of course, I could. I knew what must have happened. There could be no other logical explanation. But that didn't mean I wanted to face it.

"I do appreciate it must be tough to get your head around all this," he said, with a look of mock sympathy. "No doubt you thought I'd been dumped at the bottom of a deep hole somewhere. Nothing but a rotting corpse."

"No, that's not what I thought. She told me ... she told me you'd survived, that she'd got you to the hospital in time."

He took a step towards me, his eyes glinting with satisfaction.

"Well, who would have thought it? You're actually upset." He came right up to me and put his hand on my shoulder. As much as I wanted to bolt, I didn't. I stayed there, frozen, dreading whatever was about to come next. "Don't worry. You freed me. I'll admit the last five years or so, locked in your barn with barely a drizzle of blood to sustain me, were not what I'd call ideal. But then that lovely little owl came crashing through the roof and let in the rats and mice. They were drawn to me for some reason, but instead of the food they were hoping for, it was me who had the feast. Can you imagine that, Merrewyn? Have you ever had to taste their foul blood? However, disgusting as it may have been, it was enough to give me strength. Not much, but enough to get out of there. And then, when I heard your voice talking in the car, I recognised it instantly, and followed the scent of your young man to the retail park. And what do you know, he led me to my first proper meal. Absolutely delicious. And now I think I might actually prefer this life."

I knew he was still talking to me, but I couldn't hear any more. I was staring at my mother, waiting for her to tell me it was all a mistake. A terrible coincidence. That something else had happened. That I wasn't responsible for this. I hadn't killed him.

"Mum," I sobbed.

"I'm sorry," she cried. "He already had your blood and venom in his system when I reached him. There was nothing I could do. It was either that or … or …"

"Or kill me? That's what you mean to say, isn't it, Angela? But you've far too much compassion for that, haven't you? You're far too soft hearted. It's a shame. You don't know what you're missing. It's actually quite a thrill.

"You killed them!" I choked out. "You murdered Craig and his girlfriend. And the homeless man."

"Just like you murdered me!" he spat. "You made me what I am. And yet you get to live with your family. You get to live surrounded by friends. You with your idyllic life and your little man who comes trotting along on your heels."

"No! No!"

I was determined to make him hear the truth.

"It hasn't been like that. It really hasn't. I've been on my own for years."

"On your own? Like I've been on my own? So isolated that you start to doubt whether your senses truly work anymore? Because you're hearing voices where there are none and you're seeing things in the shadows when there's nothing there? So abandoned that you gnaw at your own limbs in the hope that it will keep you going for just a day longer? No. You've never been on your own. But I will show you. I will show you what it's really like."

Chapter 40

Date: July 22nd
Followers: 32651

THERE ARE a lot of things I would like to tell you about what's happening in my life now, and some of them are good. To be honest, I've probably got enough stuff going on to start a whole new blog, but I want to get to the end of this story, and the hardest bit is still to come.

The Castle was freezing. Not for me but for my parents. I could see the goosebumps on their arms and hear the constant shivering of my dad as he struggled to keep warm, although I suspect that some of his shivering was down to fear. And I couldn't blame him. Christopher had expressed the desire to see me utterly alone, and the simplest way to achieve that would be to kill my family. At least I now knew for certain what he wanted.

It was while Christopher was ranting at me that I was aware of Glen stirring in his chair behind him. There was a large purplish-green lump on his forehead, and his hands hung down between his knees, almost to the floor. As I surreptitiously watched him, I noticed something beneath his chair. The gun. It must have landed there when Christopher ripped it out of my hand and tossed it aside.

A gasp caught in my throat and a glimmer of hope fluttered within me. I quickly looked away, aware he'd be watching my every movement. But if I could just get Glen to see the weapon, then there was a chance that I could end this. What I needed was enough time for Glen to wake up and clear his head and for Mum and Dad to work out their own plan, too.

"I can help you," I said, stepping towards Christopher.

"Help *me*," he spat. "I don't need any help. Look at me."

To prove his point, he sent his fist into one of the girders strengthening the walls and ceiling. My eyes shot up. The metal buckled, causing a cloud of dust and plaster to fall from above. The support had come away from the roof, giving me yet another thing to worry about. A positive, though, was that the noise had helped rouse Glen from his stupor.

"But you need to learn about us. About vampires. About the eighteen," I said, grasping for anything I could think of to keep him occupied.

"The eighteen?" he sneered.

I don't know why that jumped into my head. I hadn't thought about it for years. It was something my dad used to talk about when I first turned. The supposed origin of the vampires.

"My father can tell you all about them. They're a group of the most powerful vampires. The original ones. They'll kill you if you don't control yourself soon. They're probably already tracking you down after you murdered those people. They could even be on their way here now."

This was nonsense. I was making it all up on the spot, just trying to keep him distracted.

"Is this true?" he said, turning to my father.

Dad was so pale at this point, I wondered if he was going to be able to speak. But he coughed to clear his throat and lifted his head little.

"There is evidence towards an original eighteen," he started. "Powerful. Very powerful."

He could barely manage a full sentence, and to be honest, I didn't want him to. I had no idea whether there was anything to it, let alone if they kept other vampires in check, and the last thing I wanted was for him to give it away.

"I can teach you," I said, stepping towards Christopher. "I can help you stay under their radar. I can even plead your case to them, too, if they find you. Explain it was my fault. It was our fault." I gestured to my mother. "But you need to let them go. You need to let them all go, now."

The movements of his face were so minute, so minuscule they would have been imperceptible to anyone other than me. I watched with bated breath as he pursed his lips, considering my offer. I kept my eyes locked on him the whole time, trying not to look past him. Trying not to draw his attention to where Glen was now reaching for the gun, his fingers stretching towards it. I felt sick to the stomach. Christopher would be able to hear Glen picking it up and cocking it, unless I could keep him distracted.

"The thing is, Merrewyn," he said, after a pause. "I don't have any evidence that you're not making this all up."

"It's true. I promise you."

"Is it? Or is it just a way to keep me talking so that I don't notice your little brother back there going for the gun?"

He grinned as his words struck me like a punch to the stomach. He didn't even bother to look back at Glen. I shifted my gaze past him, and for the first time since entering the hall, my eyes met my brother's bloodshot ones. I gave a single shake of my head and he slowly drew his hand away from the weapon.

"Merrewyn may be lying," my mother said, straightening up. "But I'm not. I know other vampires. One who will most certainly hunt you down for nearly exposing them."

"Mum?"

Her heart was pounding fast and hard but steady. Unwavering. She was telling the truth. I knew it, and Christopher did, too. His smile grew wider.

"Well, this looks like it's news to both of us, doesn't it, Merrewyn? What a dark horse you are, Angela. I can't wait to hear all about it. But given that I only need you. I think we can dispose of the others first."

I don't know how I did it. I honestly don't. But in that instant, I knew he was going straight for Glen. If any of you wonder about a higher being, then what happened next pretty much confirmed it for me. Never in my life have I moved with such speed. I leapt across the hall. Flying past Christopher, I collided with Glen and wrapped my arms around him, plucking him from the chair and then rolling us away from danger. As I got to my feet, I sent him flying further from harm with a shove. Then I instinctively launched myself upwards, sensing Christopher would attempt to pounce on me, catching him off guard as we collided in mid-air. It was enough to send him spiralling away from my family. He crashed onto his back as I landed cat-like on all fours.

"Well, this is going to be more interesting than I first thought," he sneered at me as he picked himself up.

Before that day, I'd never been in a fight of any sort. I'd done a couple of martial arts classes at school, but that wasn't real fighting. This was. Every time his hand came for me, I was there ready to block it. I ducked and dipped and pivoted out of his way, using every part of my body to stop him from getting hold of me. But I couldn't get in an attack of my own.

"I recognise that scent," Christopher said, as he threw a punch that only just missed me, the air whistling past my ear as his fist skimmed it. "That smells like someone's been drinking fresh blood. That young man you've been with? I'd been wondering if you were holding onto him as a snack."

Behind me, my mother stifled a gasp, but I ignored it. It was taking all my focus not to get thrown into the glass cabinets. At a guess, the fight couldn't have lasted for more than a couple of minutes, but I was tiring fast, and all I was doing was dodging him. I needed something to give me the upper hand.

And that's when I saw the gun, still lying discarded on the other side of the room.

It was a split-second decision. I dived across the hall, my knees and elbows scraping on the rough floor tiles as I stretched out my fingers so far that my knuckles popped. In the blink of an eye, I grabbed the gun, twisted around, aimed and squeezed the trigger.

Chapter 41

Date: July 23rd
Followers: 33996

THE MOMENT the stake left the barrel, I realised my error. In all the practice I'd done out in the woods the previous day, I'd been aiming at a stationary target. But this one was moving towards me fast and was able to see with vampire awareness exactly what I was doing. Christopher was already meters away from where I'd aimed and, rather than hitting him square between the eyes as I'd planned, the projectile merely shattered the glass of a display case full of medieval swords and pikes.

Anger surged inside this monster I'd tried to destroy, as I frantically reloaded the gun. The air temperature was dropping as if he were able to suck the very life and heat from the room.

"You will regret that," he said.

I knew I would. I just didn't know how much. God, what happened next …

Sorry, it's not easy to write this. If only I'd been thinking straight, I would've been able to save him; I'm sure of it. Had I not been so distracted by the chill in the air and the shattering of the glass, I might have realised what was coming. But the truth was, I assumed Christopher was still after me. I was the one who'd fired the gun. I was the one who'd turned him. I was the one who deserved his wrath. But he wasn't.

With a screech that resonated through my very bones, he spun around and leapt across to where my parents and Glen were huddled. It was such a sudden movement, so fast, I couldn't make sense of what was happening, until it was too late. His hands on either side of my father's head, he gave one quick twist. That was all it took. And my dad fell to the floor. Dead.

"No!" Our voices rang out in unison.

Glen and Mum dropped to the floor beside my dad's body, their wailing instant. And me? For a second, I just stood there, not believing what I'd just seen. It couldn't be true. It couldn't. Not Dad.

I still struggle to accept it. How my life could be so utterly destroyed in such a brief moment. I wake up some days, and it's a minute before it suddenly hits me again.

Other days it feels like some twisted nightmare, and I'll go downstairs, and Dad will be there in the kitchen, getting himself a cup of tea and a chocolate biscuit. But he never is. Because he's gone. He's really gone.

Christopher turned and locked eyes with me, smiling. It felt as if I were looking into the soul of the devil himself.

"They taste better when the pulse is still going, you know, but I'm sure we could still get a decent meal out of him, if you like."

He was taunting me, saying things that would make me act irrationally, and it worked. My head was spinning. I could barely manage to see for the tears that were blurring my vision, and all I could hear was the echo of the snapping sound and my mother's sobbing.

"You will pay for this," I said, firing off another shot from the gun.

He dodged it with a casual drop of his shoulder and strode towards me. I pulled out another stake and went to reload for a second time, but my hands were clumsy, shaking so badly, it was like I was human again.

"Come on, Merrewyn. Don't make this any more painful than it needs to be. Actually, though, it should be quite interesting. I wonder if it's as painful when you die a second time as it was the first. You will let me know, won't you? I should be able to tell by how much you scream."

As he stepped closer, I stumbled backwards. I wasn't

sure how many stakes I had left in my pocket, but I knew it couldn't be many. I took aim again. This time, it hit him in the shoulder, and he winced.

"You don't really think those will work, do you? At least not the way you're firing them."

"Maybe not," I said, as he watched me reloading yet again. "But that might."

Fixated on me and the gun, he hadn't heard Glen creeping up behind him, armed with a vicious-looking pike. He plunged it into Christopher's back so hard, it burst out through his chest.

The gasp that flew from his lungs was as much from surprise as the blow itself. My eyes bulged as he staggered forwards. But if what Dad had said earlier was true, the damage to the heart probably wouldn't be enough to kill him if he escaped and had time to heal. He seemed to know this, too. He smiled again and looked towards the door. He was going to run into the night and disappear and we would be haunted for the rest of our lives—mine eternally—if I didn't manage to stop him. Not trusting my aim anymore, I tossed the gun and ran to block his escape. He came to a stop less than a foot in front of me.

"You're not leaving here alive," I said.

"You're making a huge mistake," he hissed. "This isn't how we're meant to live, like some kind of pet not allowed out to hunt. We're supposed to be great, Merrewyn. We're supposed to be superior."

"No, you're supposed to die, for good."

"Then we'll die together."

He reached out and grabbed me. I tried to push back, but he was still too strong. I could feel him pulling me towards him in some sort of sick final embrace. The point of the pike was now only inches from my chest. He was going to impale me on it and end it for both of us.

"Goodbye, Merre—"

His farewell was cut short as his head snapped to the side. As it did so, it revealed one of the stakes, embedded deep in his temple. I chanced a glance to the left and saw Glen frozen to the spot, the gun in his outstretched hands.

Christopher's grip on me loosened and I watched as his eyes rolled back before he fell awkwardly to floor, the pike still skewering his torso.

Chapter 42

Date: July 24th
Followers: 35975

SO, Glen achieved what I couldn't. He protected me, and he made sure we didn't lose any more of the family that night. Glen is the one who saved us all.

Both of us were staring at the dead vampire. Neither of us could move. Neither of us could do anything.

"Is he …?" Glen asked, eventually.

I stared at Christopher, the same thought running through my mind. How could you tell if you'd killed someone who was technically already dead? I had no idea. But I wasn't going to take any chances. I crouched down to pick up a sword, but it turned out I wasn't the only one to have that idea.

The swish of a blade slicing through the air and then through his neck, separating his head from his body. Satisfied he was really dead, Mum tossed the ancient sword to the side.

"We should get going," she said, drawing herself up. "We need to get out of here. All that noise, we're lucky the police haven't already turned up."

"What?"

I was glad to see that Glen was looking at her with the exact same expression of bafflement I must have had —clearly, she was in shock.

"Mum, we have to stop here. We'll need to explain to the police what happened."

It was her turn to look at me like I'd lost my mind.

"And tell me, what would you say to them, Merrewyn? How would you account for this? There's one man dead on the floor with a broken neck and another who's been shot, impaled and decapitated but who looks like he's already been dead for over half a decade. How do we explain that? And we need to think about you. You can't get on their radar. You know you can't."

She paused for a moment, but I'd stopped listening anyway. My gaze was fixed on Christopher, whose body, just as Mum had said, was gradually desiccating. It wasn't like you see in the films, where they explode into a plume of dust. He just looked like he'd been dead the right number of years. And, trust me, it wasn't a pretty sight.

"What about Dad?" Glen said.

"We'll have to take him with us. The snapped neck is good. It means there isn't any blood for the police to find."

The entire situation was insane. I couldn't believe what I was hearing. Yet, at the same time, I could. She was right. We daren't risk drawing attention to ourselves.

Beside me, Glen was shaking his head. From his pulse it was clear the shock was just setting in. His breathing was so shallow, it wouldn't have surprised me if he'd passed out.

"Dad's dead, Mum," he wheezed. "We need to go to the police. We need—"

And just like that, Mum raised her hand and pointed a needle directly at his neck.

Glen's eyes widened.

"You can't seriously be planning to drug me," he said, in disbelief.

"I will. Believe me, I don't want to, but I will."

He looked at me, needing reassurance that he wasn't the only one thinking the situation was utterly insane.

"I think we should all calm down a bit," I said, stepping between them. "Look, Mum, we need time—"

"You need to snap out of it, Merrewyn. We have no time. We need focus here. Now, tell me, can you hear anyone? Is there anyone outside. Security? Police? Anyone at all?"

I have never had such a problem homing in on sounds as I did that night, and when I assured her there was no one there, other than a couple of late-night drinkers passing by, I wasn't entirely certain I was right.

"Okay. The car is parked just around the back. We need to get your father there and into the boot with no one seeing us. Can you do that, Merrewyn?"

"I … I think so. Yes."

"Glen, you need to find where the recordings from the security cameras are and wipe everything."

"What?"

"You heard me. We can't leave any evidence that we were here."

"Um, it's probably stored on a cloud."

"Does that mean you could do it from home?"

"I think … I don't know."

"That's not good enough. Can you do it there or not?"

Glen nodded quickly.

"I can do it."

"Okay then. Let's get home."

I might joke about how he's my big little brother, but at that moment, he looked like nothing more than a scared child. All I wanted to do was wrap my arms around him and hide him from this awful world he'd been dragged into. But that wasn't possible.

The journey back home from Colchester with Dad in

the boot was torture. His body thudded each time we hit a bump or pothole, and his head kept knocking against the back of my seat. I don't know if hell is a real place, but it must be the closest I've ever got to it, if it is.

The moment she drew up outside the house and unbuckled her seatbelt, Mum was back in action.

"Glen, the security cameras. Deal with them straight away. It doesn't matter how much you have to wipe, just make sure you've deleted everything showing Christopher and us. You understand? We'll start dealing with the rest."

He nodded silently, having not said a single word since we got in the car. He got out and headed indoors. I suspect I was meant to follow, but I found myself unable to move, my eyes locked on Mum.

"How are you doing this? How are you not affected by what's happened? Your son just had to kill a vampire. Your husband is dead, and you're talking about covering it up like this is normal. He's dead mum! Dad is fucking dead!"

She shot me a dark look.

"You think I don't know that? I'm the one who kept that monster alive. I'm the one who hadn't the guts to kill it, as I should have done the moment I realised you'd turned him. I'm the one who has to live with this, Merrewyn. All of it. But I'll do what I have to. That's what I've always done … to keep you here."

At that point, I realised I didn't know even the half of it.

"There *are* other vampires," I said, recalling what she'd said to Christopher before Glen killed him. "You've met others like me, and you never told me."

She confirmed it with only the smallest dip of her chin.

"We'll talk about it later," she said. "Right now, you should get inside."

Chapter 43

Date: July 27th
Followers: 37721

SORRY FOR TAKING a few days to regroup after that last post, but I hope you understand why. It was tough to write. Much tougher than I'd expected. And I'm finding things so draining at the moment. With the rugby club donations, I've got enough blood to see me through for a little bit, not to mention Glen and Lovisa pitching in. But I've been out in the daylight much more lately, meaning I need more than usual, and it's a worry. I'm so fearful of what will happen if I don't manage to find a suitable alternative supply.

If I had my messages and comments open, I'm sure

more than one of you would have asked about Noah. I didn't get to the hospital for another couple of hours. Believe me, I wanted to, but I was dreading hearing that I'd lost him and just couldn't handle it. I'll get to him soon, I promise, but I'm not done with Mum and Glen yet. Not even close.

After she'd snapped at me in the car, I carried Dad inside and propped him up in the armchair in his office. I don't know why I did that. I could have laid him on their bed or on a sofa, and I nearly tripped over, trying to get him there, with all the papers and books on the floor, but somehow it felt right. As I stared at him, I could almost imagine that he'd just drifted off to sleep while reading, the same way he'd done a thousand times before.

I was just about to leave when something glinted from the wastepaper basket. As I moved towards it, it became clear what it was.

"The Heart Infernal," I whispered.

I reached in and plucked it out. As I clenched the red stone in my hand, tears burned my eyes, and somewhere in the depths of me, I wished that it would work. That this single stone would burst into life and put an end to all my suffering. But the seconds ticked by and nothing happened. I tucked it into my pocket and left the room.

Upstairs, I knocked on Glen's door. When no answer came, I opened it anyway and stepped inside.

"How's it going?" I asked, glancing at the lines of script on his computer screen

His eyes stayed fixed on what he was doing, as he tapped away on the keyboard.

"I've found their server. It's just a case of getting in and deleting it all. I'll get rid of everything from the beginning of the week," he said. "That should arouse less suspicion, don't you think?"

"I guess," I replied.

While he worked away, I stared at the back of his head. There were a thousand things I wanted to say to him. In the end all I managed was, "I'm sorry."

He paused for a split second, his hands hovering above the keys. Then the moment passed, and he was back, typing away. Another few minutes went by before he spoke.

"It's done."

There was no avoiding the inevitable. I needed to speak to Mum to find out just how much she'd been hiding from me. So, leaving Glen upstairs, I went down to the kitchen, where she was fixing herself a large whisky. Judging from the smell of her breath, it wasn't the first, but I didn't say anything. I just stared at the broken kitchen table.

When she'd drained the glass and reached again for the bottle, I knew she had no intention of being the first one to break the silence.

"You should have told me about Christopher," I said.

She finished pouring her drink before she answered.

"What good would that have done? He was already

dead, for all intents and purposes. And you were already distraught enough about having bitten him. If you'd known the whole truth, you'd never have been able to forgive yourself. You wouldn't have had any chance of a normal life."

"I don't have a normal life now, Mum. I'm dead. I'm dead, and it turns out I'm a monster, too."

"No you're not. You're my baby."

"I'm the same as him, Mum. I'm just the same."

She started shaking her head, vigorously.

"He was never like you, Merrewyn. I could tell straight away. He was snarling and vicious and trying to bite me. You weren't like that when you first turned. You had your moments, I'll admit, but the real you was still in there. No." She shook her head again. "He was never going to be saved."

I couldn't believe how calm she was, how matter-of-fact. But that's when I realised why. This was a relief to her. She'd spent the last five years harbouring this massive secret. Now she was free of it. But then I remembered something.

"What about the other vampires you know of? Who are they? Why didn't you tell me?"

"I was making it up. I don't know any others," she said, dismissively.

The glass wobbled slightly in her hand, and combined with an erratic heartbeat, I had no doubt at all.

"Stop lying, Mum. You deliberately sabotaged my

chances of finding other people like me. You deliberately kept me isolated."

She put her glass down and moved towards me, then attempted to take hold of my hands, only for me to snatch them away. Disappointment flashed across her face.

"Darling, you have to understand I did it for you. I didn't want them to corrupt you. I wanted you to have a normal life."

"I'm not fucking normal, Mother! When are you going to see that? I'm a fucking vampire!"

I was pacing now, holding my hands against the sides of my head as I tried to think straight.

"At least tell me who they were. Where did you find them? When did you speak to them?"

This time she didn't try to take my hands, just lowered her gaze.

"I will tell you. I promise," she said. "But we should probably get your brother. He needs to hear this, too."

Chapter 44

Date: July 28th
Followers: 49665

OUTSIDE, the rain is hammering down on the roof, and thick clouds blanket the sky. I used the cover to head out to the shops and fetch Glen some basic groceries. I'm pretty sure if I didn't, he wouldn't eat at all. I'm worried about him. I know, given what he's been through, it's not exactly something you can expect someone to recover from overnight, but it's been four months now. I just wish he'd talk to someone. Me, Lovisa, Noah even. Anyone. I'm so scared that he's slipping away from me. But you haven't come here to read about Glen, have you? You want to know what my mother told me. So now's the time to spill the beans on the big family secret.

I went upstairs and fetched Glen, as Mum asked. He hadn't moved from his computer, but the screen was black and his eyes unfocused.

"Mum wants to speak to us both," I said, from the doorway.

His head turned to me, but he still had that distant look.

"She wants to tell us something."

He didn't nod or speak, just rose to his feet and pushed past me, heading downstairs.

"What are you doing about Dad?" he said the instant he reached the kitchen.

"I'm going to call an ambulance shortly," Mum replied. "We just need to change a few things."

"Change things?" I asked.

"His position, mostly. I'll give him an injection—up the level of troponin in his blood. That will make it look like he had a heart attack. But we'll need to put him on the floor. Make it look like he fell awkwardly to explain … you know."

"How he snapped his neck?" I said, helpfully.

"Yes."

"Jesus, Mum," Glen said, through gritted teeth. "This is insane. You do know that?"

"I do," she said. "But you really don't need to worry

about anything. I'm the one who brought this on the family. I will sort it out."

She looked down at the now empty glass.

"This isn't going to be easy to hear," she said, "for either of you. But I need you to know I would do the exact same thing a hundred times over if I had to."

"What did you do, Mum?" I said, my eyes locked on hers. "What else is there?"

She drew a deep breath in through her nose before she spoke.

"I changed you."

Her words didn't sink in at first. They made absolutely no sense whatsoever.

"I don't understand," Glen said, voicing my exact same thought. "What do you mean, you changed Ryn? Medically?"

She nodded, and her hands trembled as she rubbed her fingertips together. Never in all my life had I seen her look like that, and it wasn't reassuring.

"Do you remember the last time you had all your bloodwork done, to check you were still clear of the cancer?"

"You mean just before I was turned? Yeah. You said it came back negative."

She stopped and looked at me, tears pooling on her lower lids.

"Oh my darling, I wish that were true. I wish so much that were true. I had seen the signs for months. The forgetfulness. The tripping over words. Losing track of a sentence halfway through it. I knew what it meant. The cancer was back. And it had reached your brain."

I shook my head, trying to remember the time before the last specialist's appointment. From what I could recall, Fin and I had spent most of it on the sofa together, watching films. It was winter, though. What else was there to do?

"You didn't see it. But I knew, and I realised how much worse it was this time. I spoke to a number of doctors, and their verdict was worse than I could have ever imagined. They gave you two months, at most."

She paused. I knew she wasn't finished, but I couldn't help speaking.

"So you decided to turn me into a vampire."

A sad smile lifted her lips.

"You can't be around your father for as many years as I've been and not have a little bit of his passion rub off on you. You know what he was like, obsessed with lycanthropes and sirens and the like, and the doctor part of me had always be drawn to the idea of vampirism. The thought of what we could do if we could harness just a fraction of what they possessed. It was purely for research purposes that I'd first started looking into it and following up leads, much the same way you and Glen did. And when I finally tracked one down that would speak to me … well the timing was so amazing, it felt like fate."

I turned to Glen, to see his mouth hanging open. If it

hadn't been for the fact that I now knew what she was capable of, I would've sworn she was off her rocker, too. I guess she was. Is. It doesn't matter.

"So, how did it work? You just called them up and said please come and kill my daughter and bring her back as a vampire?"

She looked from me to Glen and back again.

"Yes, pretty much. I mean there were other things that needed to be agreed, but basically that was it."

"What other things."

"They don't matter."

"They matter to me!"

My fist swung back and smashed into the wall. Her eyes widened and I knew her usual rebukes about keeping my temper and watching my strength were on the tip of her tongue, but she managed to hold them in.

"Just things that I should be aware of."

"Things like?"

"Like not letting you draw attention to yourself. It was imperative to her that you didn't do that, with the risk of leading someone back to her."

I drew in a lung-full of air.

"What else?"

"I've told you everything, Merrewyn."

I'd heard so much, yet I still didn't know what to think. My Mum had taken my life in her hands and decided my fate for me. As the anger boiled up, I considered why she'd done it. She'd done it so she could keep me with her. Did that make it any better, though? Surely all mothers love their children, but that wouldn't lead to them turning them into vampires.

I couldn't decide what to do next. I looked at Glen. He'd remained conspicuously silent throughout all this, but I could feel the anger simmering in him, too, although I didn't know where it was aimed. At me? Because I'd ruined his life yet again? But when he spoke, it all became clear.

"We will bury Dad as a family," he said, looking Mum square in the eye, his voice so quiet it was almost a hiss. "Then that's it. We're done with you."

Chapter 45

Date: July 29th
Followers: 51012

SO THAT'S how it is. Glen and I are on our own now. It hasn't been straightforward, mind you. Plenty else has happened.

That night, Mum called the ambulance for Dad, and we had to watch his body being carried away on a stretcher with a white sheet over it. The only thing that felt real in that moment was Glen's hand in mine, squeezing so tightly that my knuckles popped. I wish there was something I could have said to him then. Something that would have helped make sense of it all. But there was nothing.

For the next few months, we stayed at the house. Glen had his exams to do, and we couldn't afford to go anywhere else.

As for Mum, I don't know where she is, and that's the honest truth. She carried on paying the bills and dropped off a dozen pints of blood two weeks after she left. God knows where they came from. I wasn't there to ask her, which was no great shame. Trust me, I don't like talking to her. I don't even like thinking about talking to her, but Glen's even worse.

For a while I was worried that what he'd been through might break him completely, and I don't just mean the kidnapping and Dad. The way that Mum had betrayed him seemed worse than what she'd done to me, in some respects. She hadn't considered him at all. She'd been so fixated on saving me that she'd failed to see the other awesome child right under her nose. He'd just been extra baggage, dragged along in my wake and then had his entire life derailed. God, I can't imagine his pain, but I'm trying to be there for him as much as I can.

We are still left with the puzzle of the old lady who was killed the night of Lovisa's party. Clearly it couldn't have been Christopher, he was still locked up then. Maybe it was connected to me somehow, or just a coincidence. I'm not sure if we will ever really know.

At least university will be a fresh start for us both. New people and a chance to reinvent ourselves. Yes, you read that right. Glen and I are at Aberllaran together. He somehow managed to pass all his exams, and I accepted the place they'd offered me, too.

Now we've got our student loans agreed and Glen is working on appropriate accommodation for us, things are starting to come together. Sorting all this out has kept us both occupied. It's fair to say, I'm busier now than I've been in the last seven years combined. Of course, a large part of that is to do with the fact that I, Merrewyn Colt, Vampire Blogger Extraordinaire, have a boyfriend! Yes, you read that bit right, too.

Which leads me to Noah. He and I are now officially an item which means, in case you haven't already figured it out, he didn't die. Thank God. Apparently, the doctors said they'd never seen so much blood loss in someone with such an insignificant wound, but you've got to hand it to them, they did an amazing job of patching him up. According to one of the nurses, it was touch and go for a while, and his heart actually stopped at one point. But by the time I got to the hospital, about an hour after the ambulance had picked my dad up, he was out of A&E and on a regular ward.

He was asleep when I arrived, so I just took his hand and waited for him to wake up. When he finally did, I dropped my head onto his chest and allowed myself to cry a few tears of joy.

"It's okay," he said, stroking my hair. "I've got you. I've always had you."

As I sat up and wiped my cheeks, I wanted to smile,

after all he was alive, and that night could have gone so much worse. But seeing him survive, somehow deepened the sadness of the loss of my dad. But he didn't ask me what had happened. He just held me.

They discharged him a couple of days later, fortunately in the evening, and as we stepped out into the moonlight together, it was clear something had changed between us. Yet there was no need to articulate it. He'd sacrificed himself for me and my family, and I knew that was a debt I could never repay. But I wanted to. I still do. The good thing is, I've got plenty of time to try and make it up to him. I started by insisting he come and stay with me and Glen while he got his strength back.

"There's one thing I need to show you before we go home," he said, as we climbed into the back of a taxi.

He leaned forwards to speak to the driver.

"Can you take North Hill Road, please, mate?"

The man nodded.

I wasn't worried. After all that we'd gone through I knew that, with him, I was the safest I could hope to be, emotionally at least. We drove out of the hospital, taking a left towards the Castle. I closed my eyes yet was unable to stop the image of Dad's neck snapping from replaying in my mind.

"We're on North Hill Road now," the driver called over his shoulder.

"Great. Could you just pull up … here?" Noah said and opened his door. "We'll just be a minute."

"What are we doing?" I asked, getting out.

"Look." He pointing to the shop in front of us.

It was a fish and chip shop, and above the front window was the name.

"*The Miserable Mermaid,*" I read aloud.

And below that, in the window, was a handwritten sign that read: Opening Soon.

"There's more," he said, with a smile.

He took my hand and led me to the side of the building, and there, on the bare brick wall was an enormous mural. It was an underwater scene with exotic fish, a sunken galleon and, right in the centre, a rather unhappy looking mermaid. There was something vaguely familiar about her. The shape of her eyes and the purple hair.

"Is that supposed to be me?" I asked, with mock indignation.

"Jesus, Ryn, the whole world doesn't revolve around you!"

I reached up and kissed his lips. It was a much more PG-rated moment than I would have liked right then, but I was conscious we were in public.

"I don't want you to ever think you can't trust me," he said. "You always can. And I'll be here for you. If you want me, that is."

"I do," I said, reaching up onto my tip toes and kissing him again. "Now, let's go home."

So that's it. You're up to date. For now. Curious as to how having a boyfriend works when you are a vampire? Or what university will hold when Glen and I start over? And just wait until you find out who else is there. **Make sure you keep following along in Bloodsucker's Blog: Love Bites now!**

SCAN ME

In **Bloodsucker's Blog: Lost Souls** we see Collina start to reveal her kindness. Ever wondered what she was up to before she turned up on Ryn's doorstep. Claim your short story Bad Blood to find out now!

You'll also get all the latest news about updates and releases.

Note from Ella

First off, thank you for taking the time to read **Bloodsucker's Blog: Life Sucks**, Book 1 in the Bloodsucker's Blog Trilogy. If you enjoyed the book, I'd love for you to let your friends know so they can also experience Ryn's crazy journey. I have enabled the lending feature where possible, so it is easy to share with a friend.

If you leave a review **Bloodsucker's Blog: Life Sucks** on Amazon, Goodreads, Bookbub, or even your own blog or social media, I would love to read it. You can email me the link at ella@ellastoneauthor.com

Don't forget, you can stay up-to-date on upcoming releases and sales by joining my newsletter, following my social media pages or visiting my website www.ellastoneauthor.com

Acknowledgments

First off, thank you to Orina for her amazing covers for the whole series and Carol for her diligent editing.

To Lucy, Kath and all the proofreaders who have helped hunt down those pesky and ever elusive typos.

To Beba and the rest of the Beta Readers for all their feedback and support.

And lastly, thank you to all of you readers out there for taking a chance on my book. I hope it has bought you as much joy reading it as it did for me writing it.

Made in United States
North Haven, CT
24 December 2023

46565690R00167